Images of Authority

The Terry Lectures 1964

OTHER COMPASS BOOKS

Apologetics and the Biblical Christ
AVERY DULLES, S.J.

Bishops: Their Status and Function
KARL RAHNER, S.J.

The Church is Different
ROBERT ADOLFS, O.S.A.

Light on the Natural Law
ILLTUD EVANS, O.P. (Ed.)

Man and Wife in Scripture
PIERRE GRELOT

Man at Play, or, Did you ever Practise Eutrapelia?
HUGO RAHNER, S.J.

Mary's Place in the Church
RENE LAURENTIN

Mutations of Western Christianity
ALBERT MIRGELER

Primitive Christian Symbols
JEAN DANIELOU, S.J.

The Variety of Catholic Attitudes
THEODORE WESTOW

Images of Authority

A Consideration of the Concepts of *Regnum*
and *Sacerdotium*

by J. M. CAMERON

COMPASS BOOKS

LONDON · BURNS & OATES

BURNS & OATES LIMITED

25 Ashley Place, London S.W.1

First published in Great Britain, 1966

The poem *"Regnum* and *Sacerdotium"* first appeared in *Poetry and Audience* (Leeds).

Printed in Great Britain by
Northumberland Press Limited
Gateshead

Contents

Let every person be subject to the governing authorities. For there is no authority except from God, and those that exist have been instituted by God.

The Letter of Paul to the Romans 13:1

Thou hast seen a farmer's dog bark at a beggar? . . . And the creature run from the cur? There thou mightst behold the great image of authority: a dog's obeyed in office.

WILLIAM SHAKESPEARE, *The Tragedy of King Lear*, iv.6

Preface

THE lectures which constitute this small book were originally given in the autumn of 1964 to an American audience at Yale University. The text bears some traces of both the occasion and its setting and I have made no attempt to remove them. Had I been speaking to a European audience some of my examples would have been different but I should not have wished to make any changes of substance. In what I had to say about contemporary martyrdom I should no doubt have mentioned, not the three civil rights workers murdered in Mississippi, but the name of Franz Jägerstätter whose wonderful example and glorious martyrdom have been so well described for us by Dr Gordon Zahn in his study *In Solitary Witness* (Holt, Rinehart and Winston, 1964).

In the lectures I have tried to elucidate what I take to be the central notion and puzzle of Christian politics: the belief that supreme authority in Church and State is vicarious. My contribution is in intention to the *aggiornamento* of Christian thinking so much desiderated. The lectures were given before the discussion at the Second Vatican Council on civil and religious liberty and before the matter was voted on. I am indeed happy that some of my conclusions can no longer be thought bizarre, as coming from a Catholic, but are on the contrary in harmony with the most recent expression of the *Magisterium*. Some of us have always believed in civil liberty and toleration on grounds of principle and not as a matter of expediency but we have been troubled by the thought that an honest witness to our belief might at particular times and in particular places have brought us into a tragic conflict with ecclesiastical authority. What has now been decided at the Council is much more than an elucidation or development of doctrine. No man of sense can honestly believe that the formal repudiation of an idea of the right relation between Church and State and of the duties of Church and State in relation to orthodoxy and heresy that is as old as Constantine and is supported by the authority of Aquinas and other doctors of the Church is properly to be described as no more than the rectification of a misunderstanding. An infamous chapter in the history of Christianity has now been closed, not without some agony of spirit.

To be asked to give the Terry Lectures at Yale is both an honour and a piece of good fortune. The hospitality of the University was for me a memorable experience and I take this opportunity to express my gratitude to all those who combined to make my stay at Yale so agreeable. No one at Yale will be offended if I single out for special mention Reuben A. Holden who was responsible for arranging the details of my stay. Yale is well served in many ways, but it is in nothing more fortunate than in having Mr Holden as its Secretary.

I am grateful to Mrs Jane Isay of the Yale University Press, who prompted me to remove many infelicities and obscurities from the original manuscript.

My best thanks are also due to the University of Leeds for granting me the necessary leave of absence.

J. M. Cameron

University of Leeds
October 1965

Regnum and *Sacerdotium*

TO THE MEMORY OF GEORGES BERNANOS

To see him standing in snow before the priest
is like watching a Chinese funeral
(there they don't know this fight of serpent and crocodile,
there they have great dragons and tease them with fireworks).

Between dark woods a river of scarlet
springs here, springs now, trumpets for the blind,
flags stiff with bars of gold, buckramed with blood.
Gold lacing binds the scarlet and the black,
gold for the leafy domes, for rings, for
bruit de l'argent autour de l'autel.

Underground, a sewer, sluggishly now
it laps the feet of Monsieur Homais who
with a withered hand dispenses prophylaxis
against the resurrection of the just.
How can the tombs break when the interchange
of blood and night is the bed of love
the ladder leaning by the proud window
the severed head clasped to her breast
(among the mountains a slice of rhetoric)?

Ni moi, ni Péguy.
                            Right. Under the moon
you spied the graves, turned on a spit
all those in red and black whose golden names
were chiselled in the rock. Now the charred rags
are sodden with your phlegm.

Images of Authority

All the same, something was not quite purged.
Would you have flushed the Drumont from your bowels
had there been time?

                    (For example, between ourselves,
the Jews were at the beginning of this business,
scarlet and black were laced with gold, gold
for domes, for rings, for altars, still was gold.
Yes, that was how it was.)

                  Cher Maître,
as to the Jews, that's how it had to be,
that's how it is. For curling round the Cosmos
the son of David marched, settling his kingdom.
Careful as any *Schnorrer* was this young prince,
numbering his cattle, crazy if only one
was missing at the count. After sunset on Friday
he stays in the shadow by the synagogue wall
and watches all the Sabbath for his father.
On the first day of the week he finds him.

Then the gold, the scarlet, the black,
the trumpets, the fireworks, the flags,
are all for him: no longer black for death
and black for priests, and black for priests and women,
no longer scarlet for royal concupiscence,
no more the serpent and the crocodile
twinned, twined in fire and sullen night.

Priesthood is for minutes and hours,
days and years. The king shall rule for ever.

That's how it is. That's how it has to be.

I

Vicarious Authority

THE conflict between the regal and the priestly power almost destroyed medieval society and provided a staple topic for its political theorists and its lawyers. This conflict no more exists, at least in an overt form, in modern society than it did in the society of the ancient world. No one doubts that in the purely legal sense the State is omnicompetent, and that if and when the command of the State is resisted on grounds of conscience or of interest, there is no body of recognized rules to which a cogent appeal can be made. Certain provisions of the Code of Canon Law forbid the bringing of an ecclesiastical person before a secular court; but even in those states that affect to be governed by a regard for the rulings of the Roman Church, such provisions may be heeded as a matter of policy but are never treated as a matter of right. The apparent counter-example provided by those states in which relations with the Church are governed by concordats is not really a counter-example; for a concordat no more infringes the sovereignty of that state which concludes it than any other treaty with another state.

The essence of the medieval conflict—as distinct from such conflicts as may exist today—was that it was a genuine conflict of jurisdiction for which there were in certain particular and crucial cases no normal, accepted means of legal settlement. There is an objection to saying that the conflict was between two distinct societies each having its own legal system, since the membership of the one was virtually identical with the membership of the other; Jews and pagans did not count as members of either society, but as subjects. Further, the legal system of the one was, both in practice and in theory, inter-mingled with that of the other. In both, Divine law, revealed and natural, is taken to be the ultimate norm. The desperate remedies of such thinkers as Dante, Boni-face VIII, and Marsilius, remedies which may be con-strued as proposing a total absorption of the one system by the other, are extraordinary because they start up against a background of belief in the fundamental har-mony of the two systems, a harmony required and imposed by the unity of a people conceived as dwelling within a single ecumenical institution.

Whether we are to speak of the conflict between the regal and the priestly power as one between two societies or as one between two sets of functionaries within a single society, this is perhaps no more than a matter of terminology. It is the existence of the conflict, under what-ever precise description it falls, that is the curious thing. It is not at all curious that conflict should come about where there is within society a diversity of functions and where different functions are associated with different sets of per-sons. It would have been strange had there not been friction between rulers and clergy, Empire and Papacy, in the Middle Ages. In any society in which priesthood is more than a civic function such conflicts will occur. But there is something deep and mysterious about the conflict between Church and State in the Middle Ages, and it has no strict historical parallel. The depth and the mystery we find in the conflict have two sources. First, the Christian *sacerdotium* is only such by identification with the one *sacerdotium*, that of Christ; and his kingdom is not of this world. (This does not mean that Christ does not reign over the world, but that his kingdom is not an earthly kingdom with an identifiable institutional structure. The Church is not the *regnum Christi*, but the sign of this *regnum*. Institutionally speaking, both Church and State exist within and under the *regnum Christi*.) Equally, for the ruler there is no sovereignty in the full sense, except that of God. On each side the view of power is that it is exercised by those who act in the name and with the authority of God; but they are vicars, delegates, substitutes, representatives. But what is produced as backing for the exercise of power also functions as a criterion for determining if and how far power is rightly exercised. The claim that a man, emperor or pope, ruler or priest, is God's deputy and acts with a delegated authority is always subject to a torturing process of verification; for the proposition *This is the command of a legitimate authority* does not entail the proposition *This is a divine command*. This can indeed be maintained in a trivial sense, but the cost is high. It can be maintained that if a given command is manifestly contrary to what is independently known about God's will, if, for example, the command is unjust or requires that some straightforward moral rule be broken, then this is not *really* a command of the authority. This is how the English legal maxim that the King can do no wrong has always been taken. Thus we have at one time the doctrine that the

King has two bodies, a natural body and a political body.[1] Foolish or wicked commands are then commands of the King in his natural body only, and they are without political validity.

That power is open to the Divine, that determinate persons stand in a particular and decisive relation to the Divine, this idea is not something peculiar to Christianity. In the earliest civilizations the ruler was simultaneously king, priest, and god. What distinguishes Christianity, even the Christianity of the later Middle Ages, from these apparent historical parallels is that the one who holds authority is himself under the judgment of Divine authority. The authority he has is not intrinsic, but sacramental; rather than possessing authority, he is possessed by it. What it means to call something sacramental will be discussed in more detail later. Here it will be enough to say that the notion of authority as sacramental is to be distinguished from the notion of authority as dwelling in the person exercising it as a kind of *mana* or magical power, and this because of the distinction, fundamental to the idea of a sacrament, between the sign and what the sign signifies, and between the sign and the effect to which it is directed. Magical power is something at the disposal of the one who holds it. The authority that goes with an office in Church or State is not at the disposal of the holder of the office; rather, the holder of the office is at the disposal of the authority of which the office is a sign. This is not to say that the holder of an office is incapable of confusing sacramental with magical authority. Of course he may; and history shows that sometimes he does.

The idea that a sacerdotal or secular ruler is exercising a delegated power and is thus a vicar is not always a clear one. It is especially not clear where the ruler in question is not the proconsul but the emperor,[2] not the pastor of the parish but the bishop. The relationship involved in being a delegate or vicar can be demonstrated in those cases where we can point to the delegate and also to the person who has delegated his power. If we are in doubt as to the limits of the delegated power we can in principle settle this by a commonplace type of inquiry. But where the power exercised by the delegate is conferred by God, or believed to be so given, then disputes over the limits of the delegated power seem hard to settle; for the very rule in accordance with which such and such men or such and such holders of offices are to be identified as God's vicars may also declare that the person or office-holder in question is the authority who defines the limits of his own power. It is as though the proconsul held the imperial power, that this power was supposed to be a delegated power, but that it was impossible ever to inquire of the emperor what the limits of the proconsular power were. In such circumstances we should be inclined to suspect, and with some justice, that the delegation was a fiction, that the proconsul was the emperor, and that the emperor talked about by the proconsul was also a fiction.

I have suggested that there is in principle a possible process of verification, namely, where we scrutinize the words and actions of the man holding authority in the light of principles that are independently known to have the authority of the delegating power. On a Christian hypothesis, it would see prima facie to be clear that a man who enjoyed, as ruler or *pontifex maximus*, a delegated power would be going outside his delegated authority if he were to commend lying or murder or the practice of polygamy. This is not so simple as it sounds, for of course there may be a question as to what is to count as lying or murder, or even polygamy, and it may be that the authority in question claims the right to decide what is so to count. This is certainly claimed as a matter of course by all secular governments in connection with the waging of war or the execution of criminals. Neither of these, it is held, falls under the prohibition of murder; and statements made in time of war with the intention of deceiving the enemy and legislation permitting a divorced man to marry again are not commonly thought to fall under the prohibitions of lying and polygamy. There is sometimes confusion on this point, as when people say: Of course, it's wrong, but in the circumstances one has to do it. *Salus populi, suprema lex*. If we don't do it, the others will. In an ideal world one wouldn't act like this, but as things are . . . And so on and so on. The confusion is this: If I commit myself to the view that X is right (wrong), then I commit myself to the view that X may be done or ought to be done (ought not to be done); and I cannot therefore at the same time commit myself to the contradictory of the view that X is right (wrong). Something like this confused account is suggested by those who use gloomy rhetoric about "the ambiguity of power."[3] The suggestion is that all secular institutions are corrupt. Perhaps they are. But if they are, this is just a matter of fact which provides us with reasons for scrutinizing with suspicion what secular authorities tell us or want us to do, but not at all with reasons for thinking there can be bad obligations or impracticable duties. Certainly there is nothing absurd about the concept of an incorrupt authority, even if we think that as a matter of fact it is never instantiated. Only if it were *necessary* that authority should be corrupt—but what could this mean? —could we hold with the shadow of plausibility that it could rightly enjoin us to do what is wicked or dispense itself from the precepts of morality. But there is something desperately wrong with any picture of authority that has about it features requiring us to talk such nonsense.

The difficulty in the notion that a pope or secular ruler is *vicarius Christi, vicarius Dei*, is that the delegation of authority here presupposed is necessarily quite different from any other delegation of authority, since the one who is held to delegate is God, and God is not something within the world in the way all other authorities are. This is not to say that God is not present in the world; but he is not present in the world as a man or a mountain is. We cannot point to him or say where he is not. Nevertheless, our notion of delegation is derived from our acquaintance with this phenomenon in society. The question that arises is: How much of what is entailed by our ordinary discourse about the delegation of authority is entailed by the application of the notion of delegated authority to these particular cases? It is clear that there must be some entailment, if the notion of vicarious rule is not to be vacuous in these cases. We have already seen that in one respect the case of a pope, say, or a secular ruler (conceived as sovereign) is different from other cases of delegated authority in that in the other cases we can inquire of the supreme authority whether or not the conduct of his delegate is authorized by him, falls within his delegated powers; whereas it can be held that in the case of the sovereign ecclesiastical or secular ruler, the ruler himself is the sole source of those criteria we use in order to decide how far a given exercise of power is legitimate. There is a certain resemblance here between this difficulty, the difficulty about applying the notion of delegated authority to a sovereign ruler, and the notorious difficulty advanced by Hume in connection with the application of the notions of *making* and *designing* to the relations between God and the universe.[4] In both cases, a concept which gets its primary sense from our ordinary dealings with the world is applied to situations which are unique by definition and contain features making it impossible to apply the concept in its primary sense.

Two distinguishable views are run together in talk about delegated authority in the Church. There is that suggested by those ways of speaking which identify certain authorities with the sources of their power. The most celebrated of all—*vox populi, vox Dei*—we encounter outside this particular context, but those writers who speak of the Pope's words as those of Peter or of the bishop's words as those of "the apostle" exemplify this tendency to identify authorities with the sources of their power. In neither of these instances are we presented with the supremely difficult case of delegation presupposed by the expressions *vicarius Christi*, *vicarius Dei*, but the habit of mind betrayed is the same. It is thought that in identifying the delegate we are also identifying the source of his power; and this is thought to be in some sense an actively indwelling power which manifests itself in ways that can be directly experienced. I think there may be a distinction between this view and the magical view I have already discussed; and this difference is brought out by the analogous view of icons taken by the Christian East. Bulgakov points out that in Orthodoxy there is an important distinction between the paintings on the walls of churches and the holy icons: "The icon is not only a holy picture, it is something greater than a mere picture. According to Orthodox belief, an icon is a place of the Gracious Presence. It is the place of an *appearance* of Christ, of the Virgin, of the Saints, of all those represented by the icon, and hence it serves as a place for prayer to them. . . . The veneration of holy icons is based not merely on the nature of the subjects represented in them, but also on the faith in that gracious presence which the Church calls forth by the power of the *sanctification* of the icon."[5] (It should be added that in Orthodoxy, as in Catholicism, the supreme communication of Christ is in the Eucharist, and here we find the contrary of a sensible manifestation of the Divine reality, namely, a hiding of the reality and a total reliance upon faith.) It is as though the active exercise of power itself provides the evidence for believing in its authoritative and hidden source. In the extreme forms of this view the central notion of vicariousness, that of acting for or representing another, is almost lost.

It seems to suggest that the authority is present in the vicar, rather than that the vicar represents or acts on behalf of the authority.

The second view is concerned primarily with the question of legitimacy. The question asked about the one who claims to be a vicar is not whether the authority sensibly, as it were, manifests itself in his activities, thus rendering valid with a kind of immediacy the claim that here is an authentic vicar, but rather whether the claim to be a vicar is legally valid. Does the claimant stand in the line of unbroken succession from the apostles? Was the process of election properly carried out, or was it defective through force or fraud? These are examples of the questions which arise where this conception is dominant. Also, where this conception is dominant the distinction between the person and the office is made much of, sometimes for apologetic purposes, as when some Catholic historians touch upon the career of such a pontiff as Alexander VI, sometimes as though to spare the vicar a weight that might otherwise crush him.[6]

Neither of these two views is commonly met with in a pure form. They tend to fuse, though one or the other receives greater emphasis in accordance with the needs of the moment. It is characteristic of Solovyev, suspended between Catholicism and Orthodoxy, that in discussing the role of the Papacy in the struggle against the iconoclastic heresy he should speak of "the apostolic see of Rome, that miraculous *icon* of universal Christianity."[7] Here it is suggested that the authority of Rome springs both from its apostolic credentials and from the actual and perceived providential role of the Papacy in world history. Indeed, religiously speaking—authority in the State may be another matter—the holding of one view to the exclusion of the other would seem to be extravagant. The loci of authority have to be given determinate places in the religious community, and we must therefore have rules for deciding where authority is to be found; but a purely legalistic approach to the question of authority would suggest that the ecclesiastical apparatus has a life and a dynamic independently of Grace. As Congar has written, "legalism is characteristic of an ecclesiology unrelated to spiritual anthropology, and for which the word *ecclesia* indicates not so much the body of the faithful as the system, the apparatus, the impersonal depositary of the system of rights whose representatives are the clergy or, as it is now called, the Hierarchy, and ultimately the Pope and the Roman Curia."[8] One might even say this has been the underlying issue debated at the Second Vatican Council.

The two views I have been discussing are historically associated and it may be agreed that an excessive emphasis upon one or the other is religiously unfortunate. Given the notion of a man or an institution representing the Transcendent with authority, neither view is intelligible without the other. They are necessarily connected; and only in the light of this connection can the idea of vicarious authority be vindicated.

It is a presupposition of the Christian religion that God speaks to men. The form of this speaking is diversely conceived and, since God nowhere leaves himself without a witness, we may say that God speaks to all men at all times. This is to be seen in, for example, Aquinas' conception of moral reasoning as being a sharing in the life which is God's mind: *"lex naturalis nihil aliud est quam participatio legis aeternae in rationali creatura"* (*Summa Theologiae*, Ia IIae Q.91 a.ii); and any man may feel what are called the promptings of the Holy Spirit. But God speaks to bodies of men—Israel, the Church—and through these bodies to mankind. This is what is meant by Revelation; and we may take as a sketch of the provenance of God's word to man, in this latter sense, the opening passage of the Letter to the Hebrews.

> In many and various ways God spoke of old to our fathers by the prophets; but in these last days he has spoken to us by a Son, whom he appointed the heir of all things, through whom also he created the world. He reflects the glory of God and bears the very stamp of his nature, upholding the universe by his word of power (Hebrews 1. 1-3).

That God has spoken in these ways is a matter of belief and not of knowledge, for if it were a matter of knowledge it could be demonstrated that God has spoken. But belief that God has spoken may be idle, as when a man believes that God has spoken through Joseph Smith, and it may be serious, as when a man reflects upon the history of the Jews, the apostolic preaching as it is reflected in the New Testament, and other matters of fact, and then comes to believe that God has spoken and in what God has spoken. What is it that marks the distinction between a serious belief and an idle belief? This distinction exists for the unbeliever as well as for the believer; for it is perfectly intelligible that a man who does not believe should make a distinction in respect of the seriousness of the beliefs in question and think that the belief that God has spoken through Joseph Smith is idle whereas the belief that God speaks through the apostolic preaching is serious.

There are many ways of marking this distinction, and it is unnecessary to enumerate them all. Plainly, it is idle to believe what is formally absurd, though one would have to be careful not to be too sure in a particular case. (One thinks of Tertullian whose *Certum est quia impossibile est* could easily, though wrongly, be taken to be the assertion of the credibility of what is formally absurd; and even more of Saint Paul's "to the Greeks, foolishness".) Again, if what is in question is a speaking by God at particular times and in particular places, then it would be idle to believe, if this were tied to belief in matters that turned out on investigation to be fictitious. (One reflects that what was absurd to "the Greeks" was, on the contrary, precisely the claim that God spoke through particular historical events, events of a type that were either thought to be disgusting when brought into connection with the Divine—the crucifixion of Jesus—or belonging only to sacred fictions and as such, but only as such, acceptable—the resurrection of Jesus.) Again, a belief having as a part of its content a confidence in the power of the putative revelation to bring about a change of character in bad or indifferent men would be severely tried, and might in the end be done away with altogether, if instances of such changes of character did not occur from time to time; above all, perhaps, one's belief might be threatened by the absence of changes in one's own character, though this last point is a difficult one for obvious reasons.

Now, if we believe, in the serious sense, that God has spoken "by the prophets" and "in these last days" by the one who "reflects the glory of God and bears the very stamp of his nature, upholding the universe by his word of power", we do so in a way that even the unbeliever may allow to be serious; for no logical absurdity attaches to our belief, the events through which God speaks are reasonably conceived to belong to history and there are no conclusive reasons why they should be thought to be fictitious, and the promises that "in Christ" a man may became what he cannot become through his own powers are from time to time fulfilled. It is true, the pathos of faith lies in the fact that it may be tried under any and all of these three headings. With the mysteries of faith, it may not be clear whether what is being stretched to the point of breaking is the notion of logical consistency or our finite powers of comprehension. Christians have sometimes feared the trial of historical investigation, and even if we believe today that this fear is groundless, that it is a trial cannot be denied. The persistence of evil in ourselves and in the very fabric of ecclesiastical institutions is the most severe trial of all. But the seriousness of belief is not weakened by the possibility of such trials. Rather, it is deepened in the overcoming of them, though this is not always easy. All the same, a man may look at the history of the old and the new Israel and without absurdity say with the author of the *Epistle to Diognetus*: "These things do not look like the achievements of man; they are the power of God; they are the proofs of his presence."[9]

Given the concept of revelation, then, and given that it is a part of the content of the Christian revelation that in the *ecclesia* and through the *ecclesia* the transcendent God is represented with authority, it is necessary both that there should be ways of identifying the *ecclesia* and its articulated organs as a complex of public facts and also that the Spirit should authenticate himself in the minds and hearts of the believers; both that the Church should be able to point to the written records of the apostolic preaching, which must always function as an unshakeable norm, and also that the believer should know that the letter kills; both that the Church should be definable and through definition be identifiable in time and space—in 380 the members of the Catholic Church are legally defined as those who agree with and are in communion with Damasus of Rome and Peter of Alexandria, and the Catholic religion as "the religion which tradition from Peter to the present day declares to have been delivered to the Romans by blessed Peter the Apostle"[10]—and also that such a definition, and still more, that institution which is identified through the use of the definition, should be felt to be the mask of a mystery and a scandal. It is not a piece of irony to say that the eye of faith is needed to perceive the historical connection between the *ecclesia*, the little flock, of the New Testament and the vast institution, haunted by the ghost of the Roman Empire, that is its historical appearance.

Without the witness of the Spirit, ordinarily showing

itself in the act of faith itself, extraordinarily in those charismata that continually show themselves in the Church and have done so since apostolic times (especially the charisma of prophecy), the rules for identifying such and such a body as the authentic bearer of revelation would be purely formal and lacking in seriousness. But without these rules faith would be without content, for it is through the possibility of identifying the authentic tradition and the bearer of it that faith can be articulated and its content communicated. It is clear that there will always be a certain tension between the Church as a juridical institution and the charismata that manifest themselves in such a way that those who have them may transcend, so to speak, their role in the hierarchical structure. History offers many examples from the earliest times. Paul resists Peter to the face; a Catherine of Siena rebukes the reigning pope; Jeanne d'Arc is handed over to the secular arm by an ecclesiastical court; John of the Cross finds himself cast into prison by his superiors; the entire career of John Henry Newman is a melancholy illustration of the possibilities of conflict between the prophet and the men who form the apparatus of ecclesiastical power. Without the prophetic witness of such as these, the Church would have seemed no more than the ecclesiastical power structure described by the Grand Inquisitor in Dostoevsky's fable and would not in its temporal existence have provided a motive for faith.

We began with the puzzle that in the Church delegated authority is not open to the same process of verification as is delegated authority in those cases where the one who exercises supreme authority and the one to whom he delegates his authority are both within the world; and this because the supreme authority is that of God. We have seen that the concept of revelation requires that authority should manifest itself through institutional forms and a body of tradition, and also that there should be perceptible witness to the life these institutions and traditions are formally directed to. We may adapt to our own purposes the well-known aphorism of Kant: "Thoughts without content are empty, intuitions without concepts are blind."[11] The institutional life of the Church and the written record of the apostolic preaching are witnesses to God's redemptive activity only in so far as this activity is rendered perceptible to the believer by the word of prophecy and the present example of holiness. "Thus you will know them by their fruits" (Matthew 7. 20). Equally, the charismata find their place and meaning within the tradition that goes back to the apostolic preaching and within the Christian community in all its concreteness.

If we are to think of the sovereign authority in the secular State as *vicarius Dei*—a notion that is bound to strike most contemporaries as odd, but one inescapable for Christians—the logical puzzle is the same: God is not something within the world, and we cannot therefore in any obvious sense interrogate him as to the powers with which he has endowed his vicar. The traditional solution is that expressed with the utmost crudity by Blackstone: "Upon these two foundations, the law of nature and the law of revelation, depend all human laws; that is to say, no human laws should be suffered to contradict these."[12] That is, the responsibility

29

of the ruler, God's deputy, to God lies in his being subject to laws, the content of which is known independently of what he may say about it. Such a doctrine does
not necessarily imply a right of resistance to the command of the ruler. Bracton may be cited: "The king
is below no man, but he is below God and the law; law
makes the king; the king is bound to obey the law, though
if he breaks it, his punishment must be left to God."[13] It
is true that there is no necessary implication here, but
there can be no doubt that such a doctrine has a general
tendency to justify resistance to those acts of government
which are held to conflict with natural rights or with
notable moral principles, and that through all the mutations of natural law doctrine, from the Middle Ages to
the eighteenth century, it is usual for the doctrine to
be conceived as entailing the right of resistance to the
commands of an unjust ruler. It is this which provides
the logical tie between the *Policraticus* of John of Salis-
bury in the twelfth century and Jefferson's draft of the
Declaration of Independence. In both, there is a crucial
distinction between a lawful government and a tyranny,
and both hold that there are circumstances in which
men may with a good conscience seek to overthrow
governments which are lawful in the purely positive
sense. The proceedings at Nuremberg after the Second
World War were extremely dubious in the eyes of many
lawyers and for a variety of reasons (some of them good).
Among these reasons was certainly the belief that the
trials could only be justified by appealing to this ancient
tradition, that is, to legal principles that (it was supposed)
had been shown to be either purely superstitious or

mistaken inferences from the "morally tinted words"[14] used by lawyers for quite technical purposes.

The tendency for the doctrine that secular rulers are God's deputies to issue in the doctrine that a lawful (in the modern sense of "lawful") government may be resisted has its importance for the present argument only because it brings out the logical pattern to which the former doctrine commits us: for the concept of vicarious power to be capable of application in the case of a sovereign ruler, it is necessary that there should in principle be some means by which the will of God may be known independently of what the ruler declares it to be. Historically the doctrine of natural law has been such a means, for in the last analysis natural law speaks to a man *in foro interno*, and this speaking is conceived, just because the deliverances of a man's mind in these matters are thought to be a *participatio* of the Divine reason, as a final court of appeal from the judgments of the external forum. The conscientious judgment of the good citizen, therefore, stands in the same relation to vicarious power in the case of a sovereign secular ruler as the witness of the Spirit in the individual believer does to vicarious power in the case of the Church. In both cases it is held that there is a means of access to that authority from which the existing powers in Church and State derive their claims to direct the judgments and actions of men. That there should be such a means is necessary if the concept of vicarious power is to apply in the two cases. If there were no such means, there would in principle be no possibility of verifying the claim to hold vicarious power, and we should have to reject the notion as empty

—a mere attempt to persuade men through the use of a social myth that earthly power has the backing of supernatural sanctions. Whether or not God is, and creates, sustains and directs the world and human affairs may be a matter for philosophical speculation and argument, though he must be a rare man who is brought from scepticism to belief by the arguments of theistic philosophers. At any rate, to argue for the existence and providence of God is not my chosen task here. Whether or not God speaks to man in the sense that he speaks to him in a historical revelation is a matter of faith. But if we take the Christian revelation as given (and I have already argued that we can do this on the ground that belief in this revelation is serious), it is not then a matter of faith or a matter of free choice how we are to conceive, at least in broad outline, the relations between men and particular authorities. These are as much matters for rational analysis as are any others; and to some of these questions of Christian politics I now turn.

A Note on the Charismata and the Hierarchical Principle

I should like to gloss a little my statement, "that there will always be a certain tension between the Church as a juridical institution and the charismata that manifest themselves in such a way that those who have them may transcend, so to speak, their role in the hierarchical structure" (p. 28). This is not a statement of natural necessity, for there is nothing strictly absurd in the idea that grace should always correspond to office. Indeed, it would seem to follow from the grounding of the Church's hierarchical structure (in its essential features) in the Divine will that grace should correspond to office. If the grace that belongs to the office does not manifest itself, this can be either because its workings are hidden but nevertheless perfectly real or because the grace that belongs to the office has been forfeited by human sin. The "always", then, of my statement rests upon the view that sin is a pervasive feature of human history and that what distinguishes the last age in which, according to Christian belief, we now live is not the absence of sin, not even the presence of grace (it is a theological howler to restrict the presence of grace to the years of the Christian era), but our living under the signs of our redemption, the sacramental signs of which the Church is the principal. These are signs of what is already accomplished, but in their reality they belong to human history and are subject to the vicissitudes of history in every respect but one, namely, that they are preserved in their historical existence by those acts of which they are the signs. To take two examples: it belongs to the divinely determined character of the present age that the Church is indefectible and that "the gifts and the call of God are irrevocable" (Romans 11. 29) in relation to Israel.

II

Regnum

It is a nice question whether or not we do well to translate a variety of terms such as *polis, civitas, res publica,* and so on by the English term "the State".[1] What is not seriously open to question is that there is a kind of institution peculiar to civilization and found—if at all— only in a rudimentary form in primitive societies, which has the special characteristic that it, and it alone, is deemed to have the authority to kill offenders against the laws and to take away their liberty, and to raise men and materials for war. This institution is what we mean by "the State", though it may not be all that we mean by the term. It is commended on the ground that to those within its rule it brings the benefits of peace and security, benefits that cannot be had by any other means. The sickness of the State, when it lacks the power to enforce its laws, is feared as a great evil; and its death provokes anarchy and with it the continual danger and fear of violent death, that evil which thinkers so diverse as Hobbes and Pascal have thought to be the worst of earthly evils, though not the worst of evils. The minimal functions of the State are taken to be the safeguarding of the lives, liberties, and properties of its citizens and the administration of an even-handed justice between man and man.

If we look at the immense variety of states in human history we may well think this account of the function

34

of the State too smooth, too easy. In any society divided by class and interest the action of the State necessarily benefits some rather than others and some at the expense of others, that is, there may often be a contradiction between the State's function of doing justice and its function of preserving the peace of a given society. Those who live under the State may, as in the ancient world, be divided into those who are citizens, those who are not, and those who are the chattels of other men. Women may or may not enjoy the rights and benefits of citizenship. In modern times we have touched the extreme point of spiritual vulgarity and have even framed societies in which the crucial distinction between those who are fully citizens and those who are not is marked by the pigmentation of their skins. On the other hand, it is in modern times that the idea has been generally embraced that the best kind of state—even, it is sometimes argued, the only legitimate kind of state—is that in which all, with trifling exceptions, are citizens and in which all have a voice in the election of the government and the framing of its policies.

It is in modern times, too, that a particular legal and political doctrine, that of sovereignty, has been elaborated. The notion of sovereignty is not absent from medieval speculation;[2] but the classic authors of the doctrine as it has been received in modern times are Hobbes and Austin.[3] Two distinct notions tend here to be run together. There is the theory according to which it is necessary in any legal system that there should be one formal authority not subject to any other authority and having the power to issue commands or to make

35

rules (assuming, as not all would assume, that there is here a valid distinction). There is also the political question as to who or what is in control of the legal sovereignty. The theory of legal sovereignty states what is held to be a logical requirement of any independent system of laws. But it does not follow from this theory, though it has often been thought to follow, that there is necessarily a determinate political authority in control of the legal sovereignty. Again, the criteria for determining whether or not a given state is a sovereign state and not a municipal authority neither determine where in a given state the locus of sovereignty is nor whether it is in fact the case that there is a determinate political authority endowed with the powers of a legal sovereign. It is unnecessary to complicate the issue by raising all the manifold questions that can arise in connection with a federal state having a written constitution and a supreme judiciary, one of whose functions is to pronounce on the meaning of the constitutional statements. I simply note that it would be very strange to seek to maintain that the United States, taken as a whole, does not constitute a sovereign state, even though there is enormous difficulty in determining the locus of sovereignty (if indeed there is one) and in determining how far those powers exercised by the individual states independently of the federal government are those of a sovereign power.

Difficulties over the nature of sovereignty pose questions of analysis, not questions of substance. It is perfectly clear that within and as a consequence of the institution of the State, rules are laid down, men are

36

persuaded or induced or compelled to obey these rules, and those who resist them are punished if their crimes and negligences are discovered. What the correct analysis of all this may be is another matter. Over this, as over the correct account of what constitutes the moral claim of the laws upon the citizen, men continue to be puzzled: a sure sign that we are faced with a strictly philosophical problem.

The mark of a wide range of philosophical problems, though not perhaps of all, is that we don't know how to state the problem in question, though what the constituents of the problem are is quite clear. To take a philosophical chestnut, we puzzle over questions about the nature of mind and the relation of the mind to the body. These cannot be questions in psychology or physiology, for either we can answer such questions or we know how to set about finding answers. Equally, there is nothing mysterious about the nouns, the verbs, the adjectives and adverbs we use in our discourse about minds and bodies, their states and activities. If we say that a man is intelligent or forgetful, that he has a deep or a shallow mind, that his passions overcome his will, or that he has a pain in his left leg—none of these statements is in itself in the least degree mysterious. Each could serve as a paradigm case of the kind of statement which is immediately intelligible. If these statements are not clear, no statements are clear. But this would be absurd. It is when we seek to assimilate these statements to others and to find in them a common logic that trouble begins. For example, we might suppose that to locate a pain is the same thing as to locate a tumour, and then be stricken with philosophic *Angst* to discover that their implications are different; or, knowing that John is in his study and that he is thinking, we might put the strange and very unclear question: Where is the thinking that John is doing in his study? So it is with the tangle of problems concerning the correct analysis of sovereignty and of political obligation.

I do not propose here to raise directly the question as to what it is that constitutes the claim of the commands of the sovereign or of the laws in general upon our obedience. That such commands, such laws, do often have a claim upon our obedience is clear enough, and in particular cases we are in no doubt over how we should justify the law (e.g. some of the laws dealing with road traffic or dangerous drugs). That laws *as such* have a claim upon our obedience or that we are always under an obligation to obey the commands of the sovereign, these things are not so clear; on the contrary, it seems clear that a law as such, the command of the sovereign as such, these do not have a claim upon our obedience; for the collocation of *The law requires X to be done* and *I ought not to do X* does not appear to be logically absurd, for we can easily find acceptable substitutions for X. It can be argued that if such and such is the law, this constitutes a prima facie claim upon my obedience, and this is in general right; but it is only right because, and in so far as, it is the standard case that a law-making authority is beneficent. (Indeed, we might be inclined to think that this must be the standard case. To the objection that there are after all totalitarian states one would reply that it is of the essence of a totalitarian state that it is

not a *Rechtsstaat* and that many of its orders and requirements cannot be brought within the class of laws.) What
it is that constitutes the claim of the law upon my
obedience in all those cases where it would be commonly
agreed that I ought to obey the law, this is not plainly
a sensible question, for there may be no one answer. It is
not evident that there must be some general ground, in
addition to any particular grounds there may be, for the
claim of the laws upon our obedience. It is true, this is
the contention of the social contract theorists according
to whom all political obligation is to be understood in
terms of the obligation to keep a promise; but the objections to this account of political obligation are well
known.

These interesting and important questions are not at
the centre of my present concerns. I mention them to
bring out how much they are matters of analysis and
not of substance. This is not to suggest that matters of
analysis are trivial; of course, they are not, for from
mistakes in analysis—think, for example, of the notorious
mistake which has led people to attribute to communities
and to the State a "general will"—can spring consequences of substance. But it is all the same true that we
may without too strong a feeling of guilt put aside many
of the standard problems in the philosophy of law and
politics that look as though they are logically prior to
some of the matters now to be discussed; for these are
matters of analysis. It is only in so far as one can understand independently of philosophical inquiry what it is
that constitutes the claim upon our obedience of this or
that law that one can engage in philosophical analysis;

the criteria for judging the correctness of any such analysis are given by what we know prior to and independently of the analysis. This is the presupposition of the dialectical (or Socratic) method in philosophy and is presumably the point of Wittgenstein's aphorism: "Philosophy only states what everyone admits."[4]

It is sometimes thought to be one of the corollaries of the doctrine of sovereignty that no question can be put as to why we should obey the command of the sovereign. Its being the command of the sovereign is the only ground for its being obligatory. This formulation is ambiguous. It can mean that obligatoriness is defined as a property of the commands of the sovereign and as the property of nothing else. But this is no more than an exercise in persuasive definition. It can also mean that the consequences of flouting the sovereign are always such that no man who knew this could rationally choose to disobey the laws. Disobedience to the command of the sovereign would then be either a consequence of ignorance or the act of a madman. But however we take the formulation, it seems clear that such a doctrine would, if it were true, make it impossible for us to hold that sovereign authority is vicarious, for it has already been established "that for the concept of vicarious power to be capable of application in the case of a sovereign ruler it is necessary that there should in principle be some means by which the will of God may be known independently of what the ruler declares it to be" (p. 31); and this leaves open the possibility that we may be obliged to go against the command of the sovereign. As we have already seen, the classic solution to the difficulty is that God speaks to

40

man, not only through the Church and the Scriptures, but also *in foro interno*, for, it is argued, "nature" provides us with a moral criterion for distinguishing between good and bad courses of action. I propose now to discuss some of the problems connected with the appeal to and use of "nature" as such a criterion.

What is meant by saying that the State exists "by nature" and that the State exists "by convention" and what distinction is intended by those who commit themselves to one or other of these positions? It is not necessary to go in for any great amount of exegesis of, e.g., Augustine or Aquinas to determine whether or not the distinction has force outside the context of ancient and medieval speculation or to show, if this can be shown, that it is relevant to those questions of Christian politics that arise when we ask what the place of the State, with its rules and commands, is in the order of creation.

No one is likely to have a difficulty over applying the term "natural" to such an institution as the family. The human family is a consequence of the long helplessness of the human infant. Particular forms of the family are another question. Different cultures display different forms; and in sophisticated and inventive societies new forms of the institution may be tried out and, through the intervention of the law, particular patterns of family organization may be encouraged or forbidden.[5] There may be reasons why we should judge that type of family structure which depends upon monogamous and life-long marriage as superior to others, but the reasoning would be persuasive rather than demonstrative. It would seem, then, that to describe the family as a "natural" institution in a given society is not to refer to its particular features but to its general function, a function it shares with family arrangements of different sorts in other societies, namely, that of looking after children during the time they are unable to look after themselves. The same might be held to apply to friendship. Particular preferences for individuals of the same species are characteristic of several animal species; and in the case of men this preference becomes of great importance and perhaps even a necessary constituent of human life. Among men it is, as a consequence of the blending of natural liking and that intellectual exchange made possible through the use of language, less dependent upon propinquity; and the forms, ceremonies, and implications of these particular preferences are immensely varied and as culture-bound as the forms of the family.

There are other forms of human association less plainly and immediately rooted in man's nature. Even Aristotle, who sees the *polis* as in some sense ministering to and fulfilling human inclinations and thus as "natural", is aware both that the *polis* is not a universal form of human association and also that particular constitutions of the *polis* are human inventions. And history has shown that the special quality of life which Aristotle thought the *polis*, and the *polis* alone, made possible, has characterized life in institutions of a very different kind. When, in the thirteenth century, Aquinas asks whether political life is natural to man or must be thought conventional (that is, something without which human life can be conceived), his answer is not that the *civitas* exists by nature (though in this matter he does not contradict the Philosopher), but that *dominium,* the rule of some men over others, is natural. What was in question was whether or not the State, considered as an institution in which some ruled over others, was to be counted, along with private property and slavery, as a consequence of the Fall, and thus conventional.

Aquinas saves both the general Christian tradition and the authority of Aristotle by distinguishing between *dominium* in itself which is, he argues, compatible with rule over free men—the free man is one who is responsible for his own actions : *liber est causa sui*—and *dominium* in the concrete.[6] In the latter case there are servile as well as free relations between rulers and ruled. Penal sanctions are attached to laws. Men are coerced into external conformity with the laws as well as persuaded by rational argument to live well. What is for a modern man the distinguishing mark of the State's authority, that it alone can kill offenders against the laws and take away their liberty, is seen as something accidental; for sin is not a part of the order of nature. It is not that Aquinas sees the State as having a natural body and a conventional carapace. All the approvable activities of the State are natural in that they are designed to serve, directly or indirectly, man's natural inclination "to know the truth about God and to live in society."[7] All are conventional as issuing from an institution having penal powers and appear to be arbitrary and frustrating from the standpoint of men in so far as their natural inclinations are weakened and distorted by sin. Of course, not all the activities of actual states are natural in the above sense. The deformation of the State by reason of sin does not simply have the consequence that what would without sin have been a matter of rational agreement between free beings is now enforced by penal sanctions. It also has the consequence that the State may act wickedly. These are tyrannical acts, and as such they have no claim upon our obedience.

The shifting of the discussion from the question whether certain institutions are natural to the question whether certain laws, principles, and activities are according to nature is a great gain, simply because the latter are less bound to particular historical situations than the former. Today this use of "nature" and "natural" may at first appear obscure. But the old use of the term lingers on in dark corners of the law, as, for example, in the use of the term "natural justice" which has not quite gone out, and in such living expressions of our everyday discourse as "unnatural vice" or "unnatural parent". The central notion is: the natural is that which is in accordance with human inclination; this is not any inclination that men as a matter of fact have, but that range of inclination that would be shown by a standard man who is taken as the norm in somewhat the same way as "the reasonable man" is taken as the norm in English law. Rational, reflective, and experienced men may be supposed to come nearer the standard than others, though in making this supposition there may and perhaps must be a certain irony; for these, too, are fools and sinners, and inclination, even in such men, is always subject to scrutiny and criticism. It is a mark of their rationality that they know they are liable to deceive themselves about their own interests and desires. What is added to that idea of the natural which comes from the ancient world is the idea that what is in accordance with and furthers natural inclination can be stated in the form of lawlike propositions; and these are conceived as the commands of God. They are not arbitrary commands, though to man in his actual situation they may have this appearance. They are rules through the observance of which man may realize his ends; and these ends are prescribed by what he is in creation and in the order of creation. They are normative because men are agents and responsible for what they do and what they neglect to do.

It has often been thought that a great many of these rules are virtually self-evident. Hooker, speaking to us from the silver age of scholasticism, gives an interesting and curious list:

> Axioms . . . so manifest that they need no further proof, are such as these, "God to be worshipped"; "parents to be honoured"; "others to be used by us as we ourselves would by them". Such things, as soon as they are alleged, all men acknowledge to be good; they require no further proof or discourse to be assured of their goodness.[8]

The man of today, even the believer, may smile a little at such confidence. He knows that the propriety, even the intelligibility, of discourse about God is commonly doubted by educated persons, that what to Hooker are commonplaces may even be thought in our culture to be bizarre. Even if we find the views of Hooker too simple, we should note that they rest upon a principle worth examining, namely, that the content and the binding character of at any rate some moral rules can be inferred from what we know about the make-up of human beings and of the world they inhabit. To vindicate the possibility of a natural knowledge of morality it is not necessary to be able to produce a complete—or even a lengthy—list of principles; but we are bound to show that, in at least some cases, reflection upon men and the world is able to elicit the content and scope of such principles and to apply them to particular cases.[9]

By what is natural in human life I shall mean that without which human life cannot be conceived. This may not in all cases give us a very clear criterion of the natural; but it is at any rate evident that, for example, eating, drinking, heterosexual relations, and the use of language are natural in this sense. Eating *escalopes de veau à la crême*, drinking whisky, exogamous marriage, and speaking English are both natural and conventional, since to eat is to eat something and to speak is to speak some language; and so on for the other cases. It is conventional that we eat the dishes we do, speak the languages we do; but not that we eat and that we speak in a language.

Natural activities prescribe, so to speak, their own norms. We eat and drink to nourish ourselves and to procure the pleasures that go with these activities; we speak to convey information, to give commands, to make promises, to delight ourselves and others in forms of verbal play, and for many other ends. Gluttony and lying are thus contrary to nature. This does not mean that gluttony and lying necessarily go against particular human inclinations at particular times, but that they could not be norms for human conduct. Gluttony could not be the norm because its harms our bodies. If a man were to say that he goes in for harming his body as a matter of settled policy and prescribes this to others, he would not be saying something shocking but intelligible; he would be saying something that would be bound to seem without point. Of course, he could give it a point by expounding some theory of asceticism; but either this would be to explain why his case was exceptional or it would be to advance the view that what harmed his body did not harm him. If there were any reason to take as true the metaphysical view presupposed by this latter position, we should have to agree that harming one's body was not wrong and might even be beneficial; but I take it that few will quarrel with the view that it is and has to be the standard case that harm to my body is harm to me, even though we can allow that there are cases where harm to my body has to be accepted as the price of something else, as when I am called upon to suffer, for the sake of justice, physical harm at the hands of the wicked. Lying could not be the norm for purely logical reasons, since the point of telling a lie is that it should be taken to be the truth and this could not happen unless truth-telling were the norm. Further, if lying were the norm, it would not count as what we now call lying. If it were common to say not-p where we now say p, then to say not-p would mean what we now mean by p. While these considerations may not in themselves, without further argument, be enough to show that temperance and veracity are moral virtues, they suggest that intemperance and mendacity *could not* count as moral virtues. What is to count as a virtue is not in all cases a matter about which we are free to choose. Any theory of morals which rests upon the view that all moral principles are matters of choice must be wrong.[10]

It may be objected that considerations of this kind yield rules of expediency rather than moral rules. I do not think this objection is easily disposed of, but some at least of the objections included under this general heading are specious.

The argument may go like this: if one desires health of body, one will be temperate; if one desires to be understood by one's fellows, one will speak the truth. But that health of body or being understood by one's fellows are good states of affairs, these are matters of evaluation. It may be a fact that most people, at least on reflection, want health of body and understanding with their fellows; but this is all it is; and its being the fact does not *entail* the value judgment expressed by saying these are good states of affairs. To commend X is to go beyond saying that X is desired. Again, we may argue, following Kant, that it is distinctive of the primary imperatives of morality that they are categorical and not hypothetical. To suppose that there is a necessary connection between something's being right and the satisfaction of desire is to fail to see that fundamental moral judgments must be impartial and disinterested; it is in fact a crass failure to understand what morality is. Finally, it may be argued that while in general it is in our interest to be temperate and to tell the truth, to tie

48

morality to interest is to neglect, just those crucial, particular cases where to act rightly is not in our interest or is even against our interest; as, for example, in such cases as where gluttony would not seem to matter since we know we are to die tomorrow or where to speak the truth is to risk popular censure, imprisonment, or death.

These—especially the last—are powerful objections to the use of "nature" as a moral criterion. Unless we could see ways, at least in principle, of meeting them we should have to abandon the criterion.

We may expand the first objection in the following way: To say that bodily health is a good thing and is one of the things we ought to pursue is to make an evaluation. That most people do, other things being equal, desire it, does not constitute a logically coercive reason for this evaluation. There is no way in which a man who maintains that bodily health is an evil can be shown to have erred in his reasoning. If a man takes as a first principle of his moral system that health is evil and sickness good he is in a logically impregnable position. Moral reasoning must end somewhere; and it ends with moral principles for which no further reasons can be advanced. They are ultimate; and if we ask how a man comes upon his ultimate principles, the only answer possible is that he chooses them. He can give no moral reasons for his choice, for all moral reasons are either ultimate moral principles or are derived from them. If we could give moral reasons why we should hold a given principle, this would mean that the principle in question was not ultimate, but derivative.

We may grant, what is surely the case, that there are many moral principles which are ultimate in the sense that if we are asked why what they prescribe or forbid is good or bad it is not immediately clear what further information is being asked for. If a man were to ask why we should keep our promises or refrain from wanton cruelty, avoid gluttony and drunkenness and care for our children and our parents, respect in others those liberties we ourselves enjoy, and inhibit the impulse to speak maliciously about our neighbours, we might suppose him to be asking what benefits follow from observing these prescriptions and prohibitions. But if we discovered that he knew very well that in general observing them had consequences that most people in general approved of and that what he was asking was what *additional* reason there was for thinking such principles binding upon us, we should scarcely know what to say. They are not self-evident in the way that it is self-evident that if *X* equals *Y* and *Y* equals *Z*, then *X* equals *Z*, for no formal rule seems to be violated by such expressions as *wanton cruelty is a virtue* or *promises do not bind*. But there is something odd about such expressions; and if a man were to persist in using them and were then to explain that he had chosen these as first principles of his morality, we should be inclined to say, not that he had a different morality from the rest of us, and one that could only be faulted as a morality if he was inconsistent in developing his principles, but that he was a man of bad principles. It seems doubtful that men ever do advance or even presuppose first principles of this kind. Instead, they explain that particular bits of conduct seeming prima facie to violate some commonly accepted moral principle do not do so, either because the apparent subject matter is not what we suppose or because the conduct in question falls under some moral principle of superior authority. For example, ancient and modern apologists for the various forms of slavery may argue, as Aristotle did, that the person enslaved (and this would apply to every servile relation from chattel slavery to that relation between rulers and ruled where the rulers censor the provision of information) is not really a mature human being and must therefore be treated as we treat young children or idiots. Those who seek to justify torture or the massacre of the civilian populations of enemy states may argue that what is in question is the safety of the State and that this is the supreme moral principle. It would have been open (on the moral theory we are criticizing) to the German National Socialists to have maintained that belief in the rightness of propagating a false racial theory was belief in an ultimate moral principle. Naturally, their argument was that the racial theory was scientifically justified, not just chosen as a postulate of their moral system; for even men so depraved as these knew that *choosing* would not do the job.

But why not? Let us suppose that the answer is as follows: given what human nature is and what human society, if it is to be possible, must be; and given how the world in general is—fire burns, knives cut, cold freezes, a dry heat parches, what goes up must come down, and the rest—what is to count as a virtue or a vice, what is to count as a good act or a bad one, these are not matters about which we are free to choose.

Having a virtue, for example, enables us to procure some good for ourselves or for others. One who argues (supposing there to be such a man) that cruelty, for example, or mendacity is a virtue is committed to saying that the cruel or the mendacious man—not, of course, the individual cruel or mendacious man, still less the man who is on occasion cruel or a liar, for to maintain that cruelty or mendacity is a virtue is to maintain something quite general—is well-equipped to procure a range of goods that the man who lacks this virtue is unable to procure. But what could these be? Could we count what cruelty or mendacity tends to procure good? If we are known to be cruel, men will avoid us, and if we are known to be liars, men will not trust us. Could it be the case that men would count these characteristic achievements of a cruel or mendacious disposition as good things? Isn't it rather that what cruelty and mendacity are *as dispositions* constitutes their being vices and not virtues? It is not the case that to call something a virtue or a vice can be analyzed into, on the one hand, the giving of a factual account of the disposition and the conduct that would exemplify it and, on the other, the making of a value judgment which can in principle be approving or disapproving. We could not say what a society in which mendacity and cruelty were virtues would be like. In the former case, there could be no such society; and in the latter the necessary connection between "bad" and "harm" would be broken, with the consequence either that we could not teach people the meaning of "good" and "bad", or that the rules of "good" and "bad" would be reversed so that it would prove impossible to teach anyone that cruelty was a virtue, since in teaching him that cruelty was what was called "a virtue" one would be teaching him that cruelty was what in our language is called a vice. Again, we could not say that killing harmless people was an innocent or a good act simply by choosing a moral principle that would make it so, for no man could want human life to be conducted in this way, that is, no one could *think* such a morality. Of course, one could speculate about the consequences of the adoption of such a principle. But this would not be "to think a morality", for moral thinking is always with a view to action.

The second objection is that to base morality upon natural inclination and, in general, upon how men and the world are in fact constituted is to blur the distinction between morality and expediency, to exclude the categorical imperative from ethics. My brief answer would be that the contrast between the right and the expedient is either the contrast between what, taking short views, we should like to happen and the more solid goods we should on reflection prefer; or it is an unreal distinction. The contrast between the expedient and the right or the just is often made in such a case as that of the unjust condemnation of Dreyfus. One of the arguments here was that at stake was the prestige of the French Army and, as a consequence, the safety of the State; and that the fate of one man could not outweigh these considerations. This seems a confused position. Either it is being argued that to keep up the pretence that Dreyfus was justly condemned is right, in which case the distinction between the right and the expedient is removed, for what is now maintained is that there is no moral rule requiring us to treat a man justly where the interests of the State are in question; or it is being argued that to treat a man justly or unjustly is a matter of choice, and here again the distinction between the expedient and the right is not made. In any case, either the distinction between the right and the expedient is one which simply applies to those cases where, for some immediate advantage, we do what is wrong, and there could then be no question of a moral preference, for to maintain this was a moral preference would be to maintain the quite unintelligible position that in general it is a good thing to act wrongly where this suits our short-term interests; or the distinction vanishes. Either prudence and justice are both virtues, and if this is so they cannot come into conflict;[11] or justice is not a virtue at all, as the Thrasymachus of Plato seems to have argued.

There are great difficulties in determining exactly what it is that Kant has to say on the subject of ethics in general and of the categorical imperative in particular. A chief difficulty is that the formal requirements for an act to be in accordance with the categorical imperative are such that we could never have sufficient criteria, in our own case or in that of another, to determine whether or not a particular act was or was not in accordance with the categorical imperative. It may be that this shifting of ethics to the level of the transcendental is designed to safeguard what is, I am sure, crucial to the understanding both of the philosophical problems of ethics and of what morality involves: that morality has in the last resort to do with "inwardness", with what a man makes of himself apart from all worldly calculation. I feel unable to give a correct account of what this is, except to say that this, and not a utilitarian view, is what Plato attempts to establish in the discussion of Justice in *The Republic*.[12] Such a view is not at all incompatible with the view that it is a necessary condition for something to count as a virtue that it should in general tend to bring about results that men, from their natural constitution, are inclined to want.

A substantial point in connection with any account of ethics which makes the notion of imperative or command central has been well put by Miss Anscombe:

> It is worth remarking that the concepts of "duty" and "obligation", and what is now called the "moral" sense of "ought", are survivals from a *law* conception of ethics. The modern sense of "moral" is itself a late derivative from these survivals. None of these notions occur in Aristotle. The idea that actions which are necessary if one is to conform to justice and the other virtues are requirements of divine law was found among the Stoics, and became generally current through Christianity, whose ethical notions come from the Torah.[13]

The same logical point is made by Hobbes. He argues that the (moral) laws of nature are dictates of reason; and adds: "These dictates of Reason, men used to call by the name of Lawes; but improperly; for they are but Conclusions, or Theoremes concerning what conduceth to the conservation and defence of themselves; wheras Law, properly is the word of him, that by right hath command over others. But yet if we consider the same Theoremes, as delivered in the word of God, that by right commandeth all things; then they are properly called Lawes."[14] The question as to how far moral rules can be understood as laws which bind categorically arises only within the Judaeo-Christian tradition, with its view that men are the creation of a personal God who "by right hath command over" them. That what he commands is in their interest follows analytically from what God is, though in a particular case this is bound to be a matter of faith and not of knowledge, since the tie between what God requires and what God is must remain for us a formal requirement apart from faith. That obedience to God's laws should be linked with natural inclination follows from what, for faith, man is in creation : a being inclined "to know the truth about God and to live in society".

The last objection to the tying of moral rules to human interests and desires is that the stringency of what is rightly called a moral rule shows itself in precisely those cases where to observe the rule is to go against our interests and desires, so far as these can be determined at the time of judging. For the Christian no practical problem arises, for the reasons given above. But we are concerned with the justification of the use of "nature" as a criterion in morals.

If a man understands what a virtue is, he cannot but desire it, even though, if he is a bad or a weak man, his desire may seem to him idle, since he supposes he is incapable of acquiring the virtue in question. Nevertheless, he doesn't deny that he would be a better and a

How are you all? Has the new baby
arrived yet?

Len—Kram
James

happier man if he had the virtue he lacks. Now, to have a virtue is to have a steady disposition to act in certain ways when the appropriate circumstances come along. To calculate advantage in the particular case and to act in accordance with one's calculation is not to have a moral virtue, but to put oneself under a different kind of rule and one from the observance of which no steady disposition could be established. Virtuous acts are not governed by their immediate consequences but by their general tendency to further human good.

To make particular circumstances the grounds for an exception in one's own case would be to fall away from the virtue in question. Hobbes makes the point clearly: "That which gives to humane actions the relish of Justice, is a certain Noblenesse or Gallantnesse of courage (rarely found), by which a man scorns to be beholding for the contentment of his life, to fraud, or breach of promise. This Justice of the Manners, is that which is meant, where Justice is called a Vertue, and Injustice a Vice."[15] A man may say that we have still not met the difficulty of the case in question. Here, to put it in the most extreme way, is a case where to act in accordance with a virtue, that, say, of justice, is to bring death and disgrace upon oneself and (perhaps) one's family. Could there be in this case a sufficient reason for choosing to act justly? It is not perhaps enough to say that either one seeks to possess the virtue of justice, knowing in advance that to seek to have the virtue without its incidental roughnesses is not to seek the virtue, or one does not. Nor is it enough to show, what is certainly the case, that for social life to keep a certain level of decency it is necessary that, some people should be always ready to act virtuously in just those cases where to act thus is to go against all worldly advantage and even to invite what would commonly thought to be disaster. In the last analysis we are forced back upon what a man becomes inwardly as a result of his choices. If anyone wishes to deny that "this is the greatest choice both for life and beyond it",[16] I do not know that there is anything to be said to convince such a man that he is in the wrong.

Perhaps all arguments in this field have to be persuasive rather than demonstrative. If the arguments I have given are persuasive, then this is enough; for no arguments can be thought persuasive if the counter-arguments are demonstrative. The non-naturalistic theories of ethics now fashionable all claim to be demonstrative rather than persuasive; and they are such that if they are not demonstrative they have no claim upon our attention, since they seek to maintain what the *consensus humani* finds paradoxical and repugnant. One could say this was so much the worse for the *consensus humani* if the non-naturalistic arguments were clearly demonstrative; but we have seen there are good reasons for thinking they are neither demonstrative nor, in the last analysis, intelligible.

Before I return to the topic of vicarious authority and explain what I take to be the relevance of the discussion of "nature" as a moral criterion to it, I should like to mention one way in which it is useful to retain the distinction between what is in accordance with (or against) nature and what is in accordance with (or against) convention.

The distinction enables us to avoid the awkwardness

that goes with the following positions. One position is to treat matters that are plainly matters of convention, of human contrivance with particular times and situations in mind, as though they were matters of moral principle. Men have so treated the economic devices of a market economy, for example, or established social hierarchies, or the social and economic subjection of women. The other position is to treat all issues that are prima facie moral as though they were matters of convention. Examples here would be the principle that men can only be punished for breaches of established and known laws, or the principle that prisoners of war may not be killed or tortured, or the principle that freedom from coercion is a necessary condition of a valid contract between individual persons. All these principles may be established and protected by laws or conventions in particular societies; but their binding character springs not from their being conventional but from the character of the situations to which the principles apply. We feel the awkwardness of both positions, and it is useful to see that there is a way of avoiding the awkwardness.

When all this has been said, it remains true that for man in history and for us, as men of our own time, the criterion of nature is rather a guide to the character of morality than a ready and easy means of settling what we ought to do in particular situations. We cannot reasonably suppose that we are free from the moral blindness of men before us—think how many good men have seen nothing wrong with chattel slavery and judicial torture, how many Christians have seen the killing of heretics as a duty—and we have therefore no grounds

59

for going in for the romanticism of so many rationalists who have supposed that we have only to use our intelligence to draw up lists of crisply worded natural laws and natural rights and (more importantly) to apply these to concrete situations. More, even where almost everyone concurs about a given end, as, for example, that in the rich societies of the West we have a primary duty to remedy human destitution, much of what is proposed as a means to this end is a matter for technical appraisal and not for primitive common sense. Primitive common sense suggests that the budgets of states should be balanced. That there is a fallacy in the implied comparison between the accounts of a community and those of a private person can be known only if one masters a certain amount of difficult economic theory.

To say only this would be only to say that life is complicated but one must do one's best. This is bound to seem a jejune remark to any mature person, who will rather agree with Newman that

to consider the world in its length and breadth, its various history, the many races of man, their starts, their fortunes, their mutual alienation, their conflicts . . . their enterprises, their aimless courses, their random achievements and acquirements, the impotent conclusion of long-standing facts, the tokens, so faint and broken, of a superintending design . . . the greatness and littleness of man, his far-reaching aims, his short duration, the curtain hung over his futurity, the disappointments of life, the defeat of good, the success of evil, physical pain, mental anguish . . . all this is a vision to dizzy and appal: and inflicts upon the mind the sense of a profound mystery, which is absolutely beyond human solution.[17]

All that I have argued is that in some cases nature can be seen to be a moral criterion and that to see this is also to see that moral reasoning cannot, at least in the cases discussed, begin from arbitrary first principles. To show that in principle nature gives us a criterion is to show that the application of the concept of vicarious authority is possible; for it then follows that, in principle, we can judge *in foro interno* whatever in the exercise of the sovereign authority goes beyond what this authority, as *vicarius Dei*, is permitted. To inflate the claims for nature as a moral criterion beyond this point would be to go against the whole Christian tradition the burden of which is that nature is not a sufficient guide. Natural inclination is distorted by sin in such a way that to act in accordance with nature is the fruit, not of our human powers, but of grace. This is at times obscured by the excessive rationalism of some Catholic theologians who speak as though a purely natural virtue were more than a theoretical possibility. All actual virtue is (I would argue) a sign of the presence of grace; and if virtue is found, to our parochial astonishment, among the Chinese (to speak as though one were living in the seventeenth century and reading the Jesuit despatches from China), then the conclusion entailed is that here, too, the economy of grace is operative.

If we were to ask at what point, if any, in the life of politics, the rules of morality (in so far as they come under public scrutiny) would be expounded clearly, authoritatively, dispassionately, the right answer would surely be that this would come, if at all, from the mouth of a judge. There is a wonderful passage in the *De civitate Dei* in which Saint Augustine brings out at once the necessity and the tragedy of the role of the judge in human society:

How wretched, how deplorable, are the judgments passed by some men upon others in the courts of justice, even in those states which enjoy an enduring peace! Those who judge are quite unable to discern what lies in the minds of those who are judged. This is why they are often forced to put innocent witnesses to the torture, though the truth they are seeking may not concern these witnesses. . . . In this way the ignorance of the judge may be a disaster to the innocent. What is still more intolerable, something which provokes cries of horror, rivers of tears, is that a judge, seeking to avoid the condemnation of one who is innocent, should torture the accused man; and then, in and through ignorance, should bring about the death of one who, tortured and innocent, was tortured in order that an innocent man might not be condemned. . . . If the life of society is hidden in such profound darkness, will the wise man dare to sit in judgment or will he rightly fear to do so? Clearly, he *will* dare to sit in judgment. The very bonds of human society, bonds he would think it shameful to cast off, constrain him to discharge his office faithfully. . . . The good judge shows both his capacity and his human value in hating his inner wretchedness [the wretchedness which comes from his necessary ignorance], and if he understands his situation in a religious way he cries to God in the words of the psalmist: *De necessitatibus meis erue me!*[18]

It is true, the particular problem emphasized in this passage is one that arises against the special background of a legal system which employs torture as a means of investigation, and it is concerned with the necessary ignorance of the judge about what a man thinks and feels inwardly. But we may transpose the theme of the passage in such a way that the necessary ignorance arises where a judge has to decide (as obviously he has to do in those systems that come from the English Common Law, less obviously, but just as truly, in other systems) whether a given matter falls under a particular rule. Those writers who would deny that this is what a judge is concerned with, holding that such a judicial decision makes law in that it constitutes a binding precedent, forget that it is necessary to be able to speak of good and bad decisions and that not all decisions count as binding precedents—this too is a matter for the judge's decision, and is thus capable of generating the anguish spoken of by Saint Augustine.

Society is open to the Transcendent, and this implies that power and authority in Church and State are essentially representative, vicarious. Reflection upon our nature and upon the constitution of the world (both, for the Christian, belong to the order of creation) enables us in principle to sketch at least the outlines of what it is to live well. But our natural knowledge is not enough to give us clarity about how we are to live well and about the role of political authority in human life; and the course of human history is a pragmatic proof of this. What difference does it make if we place these matters in the perspectives of sacred history?

III

Regnum Christi

The most blessed martyr Cyprian suffered on the fourteenth day of September under the Emperors Valerian and Gallienus, but in the reign of our Lord Jesus Christ, to whom is honour and glory for ever and ever. Amen.[1]

THIS is how the account of the martyrdom of Cyprian, A.D. 258 ends. The wording is conventional; but it is exact in the way it speaks of the related roles of the Roman Empire and of the kingship of Christ.

It is clear from the New Testament writings that a central conviction of Christians in apostolic times was that they were living in the last age, the age that lies between the departure of the Lord from the visible earthly sphere and the *parousia*, the return of the Lord in glory. The thought of those times moved between two poles. The victory over the powers of evil, brought about by the perfect obedience of the man Jesus to his Father, has already been accomplished; and the sign of this is the resurrection of Jesus from the dead. Through these saving events mankind and (more mysteriously) the entire creation is reconciled with God. Jesus, now "at the right hand of the Father",[2] is *Kyrios*, Lord over the whole of creation and in particular he is Lord over all the subordinate powers, human and angelic, that are thought to exercise a kind of delegated power over the forces of

nature and the institutions of human society.[3] Nothing
and no one is outside the authority of the *regnum Christi*
and unaffected by its energies. At the same time, mankind and the rest of the creation are not yet in that state
of glory in which Jesus now is. This will only come about
with the parousia, the return in glory, when the *regnum
Christi* of the present age will be consummated, and Jesus
will yield up his kingdom to the Father.

It is against the background of this fundamental outlook that we must set the thought of apostolic times on
the problems of the State and its authority and of the
relations between the Church, the *laos* or people of God,
and the powers of human society. These are problems of
the interim period and are governed by the eschatological
categories through which they are necessarily seen and
interpreted. Nothing in the thought of this period formally contradicts a political theory of the Aristotelian
type; and one might argue that the idea of man as a social
and political animal is presupposed by Christian faith
and given even greater emphasis than by Aristotle, since
the cramping distinctions between Greek and barbarian,
free man and slave, male and female, are overcome. But
man perfects his nature within and through the *ecclesia*,
not the *polis*, though he lives within the *polis* and takes
up all those duties of citizenship which do not require
(as, for example, idolatry does) his forfeiting his membership in the *ecclesia*. Man's perfection does not, as for
Plato and Aristotle, rest upon an education (*paideia*),
which he shares through membership in the *polis*, but
upon the free gift of God's grace; and it is not a matter
for the here and now, for he looks towards a future state

of glory, with the resurrection of the dead and the life of the age that is still to come. Nevertheless, through his membership in the *ecclesia* he already shares in a hidden and sacramental way in the life of glory. He is baptized into Christ's death and this is his title to share in Christ's resurrection; he is sacramentally present at and shares in Christ's saving acts through his sharing in the eucharistic assembly and sacrifice. It is only with a weakening of the eschatological perspective—it can never be wholly lost so long as the Our Father is recited and the Nicene creed keeps its liturgically central position—among Christians that the theory of politics is given a certain autonomy, as in many natural law theories, just as though it were a scientific inquiry of a mathematical or physical kind, and not conditioned by the actual encounter of the Christian community with the stubborn and bitter facts of political life.

To live within the *ecclesia* as a member of it is, as I have said, to participate in its sacramental acts and in this way to share in a hidden fashion in the life of glory. The acts of the *ecclesia* are signs both of the present activity of Christ, to whom all power in heaven and earth has been given, and of what will be manifested only at the parousia. They belong both to time and to eternity; both to the life of earthly society, where nothing appears to have been changed by the redemptive acts of Christ, and to the life of faith in which everything has been changed, decisively and forever. Nothing seems to have been changed. The executioner is still taken to be the guardian of social peace. And yet there is inserted into the world an institution, a human community, in appearance not so very different from other institutions and communities and marked by the same frailties, whose essential and characteristic activities are sacramentally the acts of Christ himself. Only as this, not at all as a community living upon a set of memories and in accordance with a certain imperfectly grasped ethical tradition, this institution and community, the *ecclesia*, the people of God, the new Israel, the body of Christ, redeems the time and thus, in the eschatological categories that belong to what is central in its tradition, awaits with confidence the manifestation of the Lord in glory at the end of this last age.[4]

Now I wish to examine the concept of the Church, given in the tradition thus understood, and with it the linked concept of sacrament; to look then at the consequences of this examination for our estimate of political life; and finally to inquire what the political moral of all this may be for Christians living in our Western society.

Certainly the Church is a human society with a history, just as Jesus is a human being like us in every way except that his obedience to the Father is such that, sharing our condition, that of being alienated from God,[5] in the end he is glorified through his obedience; and this as representing the human race and thus presenting us to the Father that we may share his glory. We have to resist the persistent tendency to remove from the notion of the Incarnation its mystery, one pole of which is the genuine humanity of Jesus. If we make the humanity no more than a veil of deity, we make the life of obedience which finds its consummation in the agony on the eve of the crucifixion and the moment of dereliction on the cross a kind of comedy, with Jesus going through a performance which essentially lacks a human core. This tendency is perhaps a special temptation for those who are inclined to take pleasure in the thought of their orthodoxy. The temptation of others is to forget that they "crucified the Lord of glory" (I Corinthians 2. 8) and that "everything he does as man is an act of the Son of God, a divine act in human form; an interpretation and transposition of a divine activity into a human activity."[6] Because the Church is the sacrament of Christ, the sign which stands for and effects his saving acts for each man individually and for every generation, it expresses, sacramentally, in its historical existence, the mystery of the Incarnation; and onesidedness in the understanding of the Incarnation, the source of the christological heresies, is strictly paralleled in onesided understandings of the mystery of the Church. The Church has a perfectly human historical existence and is thus subject to all the conditions which bear upon other human societies. This is why there is nothing wrong as such in a purely scientific study, by the historian or the sociologist, of the Church in its historical existence.

But just as in and through Christ's human existence the reciprocal love of the Father and the Son is manifested, so in the Church its human existence, its acts and words, is the means by which the work of salvation is effected. And just as the glorified state of Christ is not a transcending or an abolition of his human existence, but the taking of his human nature, that nature in which he was obedient and suffered, into the life of God himself,[7] so the end for which the Church strives as a human

69

institution is also the end willed by Christ and given by the Father, a glorified human life and not a gaseous nirvana in which the flesh will be no more.

This human society, the Church, with its history, shows itself for all that it is only for faith, just because the life of glory is still to come and the saving acts of Christ are known only in a sacramental way. So far I have been using the concept of sacrament without explanation, though something of the sense of the term will have been given by this use. I will now try to give an account of the concept, important not only for a theological exposition but also for a deeper understanding of the concept of vicarious authority in the State as well as in the Church.[8]

A sacrament is a sign related to what men essentially are as creatures: as embodied, acquiring their knowledge by means of the senses, and rational, capable of speech and in this way of framing and using concepts and of harbouring intentions, of having in mind a possible future answering to a present description. Indefinitely more than this can be said about bodily existence, about the role of the senses, about the use of concepts and the relation of concept-using to language and about what it is to have an intention, but for my present purposes I need say no more than this. An example of such a sign is the pouring of water over the head of a child accompanied by the uttering of certain words. As such, the pouring of water is not a sign of anything. It has to be a deliberate act (as distinct, that is, from the accidental spilling of water), but it could be simply an act of washing or something of that kind. Now, if it is to function as what I will call, though without attaching too much importance to this way of speaking, a natural sign, it will be a sign in virtue of what it can be apart from its functioning as a sign in the particular case. Thus, although the symbolism of baptism is complex, a part of its symbolism is that it is conceived as a kind of washing, and a part of the significance of baptism is therefore established in virtue of what the pouring of water can be when it is not a sign of anything but simply the activity of washing. It is important that the sacramental sign is not only a perceptible gesture or a gesture making use of some physical thing; it is also accompanied by words uttered by the minister of the sacrament. We may say of the whole sign, the gesture and the word, with or without the use of some third physical thing, that it is in a sense a linguistic act to be construed in accordance with rules related to the community of the Church in precisely the same way as the rules of the natural languages are related to the communities in which they are used. This is why the developed theology of the sacraments has considered in such detail the question of the *intention* of the minister of the sacraments.

To say, as the theologians do, that it is a minimum requirement for the validity of a sacrament that the minister should intend to do what the Church does is to say that it is only within the linguistic community of the Church that the sacraments have their authentic meaning. To intend to do something other than what the Church does, even where much of the same gestures, forms of speech and the rest are employed, is to place what is done outside the community whose life is constituted by the sacraments and within which they are the bearers of an intentional meaning. (This is why questions of *jurisdiction* are also central to the theology of the sacraments.) To take a sacramental sign of the old Law, namely, circumcision, this is plainly not the same act when it is the ritual circumcision of a Jewish male as when it is performed as a therapeutic operation. What makes it ritual circumcision and thus a sacramental sign is that the Jewish community is the bearer of an intention with which the minister identifies himself, just as, on the side of the community, the minister of circumcision is a recognized and commissioned person. Where a part of a sacramental sign is what I have called a natural sign, as in baptism where there is a washing (or perhaps, at a deeper level, a going down into the waters and a coming out from them), as in the Eucharist, where there is eating and drinking, then this can be said to answer not merely to man's intellectual nature, as in the case of a linguistic act which is wholly conventional, but also to his whole embodied nature to which these primordial phenomena speak.

A sign points beyond itself to that of which it is the sign. The sacramental sign denotes a reality which is not perceptible in the way the sign is perceptible. Now, this way of being a sign could be something optional, a piece of pedagogy only, as when we say that something is *merely* a sign. Removing one's hat or one's shoes on entering a sacred space is a sign of this kind. The Christian sacramental signs are not, or not primarily, signs of this kind. They are said to be efficacious signs, that is, they

bring about what they signify. Further, what they represent they truly represent, not, or not merely, as the
bearers of a certain communally determined sense, but
as acts of Christ; for the Church in its acts is the sacrament of Christ just as Christ in his human nature is the
sacrament of man's encounter with God. To say that
Christ is sacramentally present in the acts of the Church,
to say, for example, with Aquinas (*Contra Gentiles*,
iv.76), that Christ baptizes or Christ absolves, is not to
say something fanciful or consoling, as when we look
at a portrait of an absent friend and say to ourselves
that it is as though he were present to us through the
portrait; it is rather to say that Christ is truly present,
but under the conditions of the age when Christ is no
longer with us in his humanity, just as God was present
to be looked upon and touched by the apostles in the
sacrament of the man Jesus, but only in this way. In this
last case there is no natural proportion between the sign
and what is signified; for that manhood can be taken
into God is known only through God's self-disclosure in
and through the manhood. The response to this dis-
closure is faith, and this is the response which all the
sacraments have a necessary tendency to elicit, even
though, at the same time, they presuppose faith in the
recipient. We may say that this tendency is *necessary*
because what the sacraments effect they do through
Christ's prayer to the Father, and this is always heard
—here is the true meaning of the much disputed doctrine
that the sacraments have their effect *ex opere operato*,[9]
and this doctrine is thus quite opposed to any magical
theory of the sacraments; and yet a *tendency*, for the

appropriation of the fruit of the sacrament, that is, grace, is dependent upon the free response of the recipient.

Given this idea of a sacrament, and given the position that the Church in its life is the sacrament of Christ, what are we to say of the structure of the Church as a visible society? How is this structure related to its sacramental reality and function?

In the first place, it is a part of the, so to speak, logic of what it is to be a sacrament that the Church, considered as a sacramental reality, should be a visible society. Next, because the Church as a society is the sacramental prolongation and application for each individual and in each generation of the saving acts of Christ, the Church is, in the sacramental mode, whatever Christ is; above all, the people of God as a whole is "a royal priesthood" (I Peter 2. 9) in virtue of Christ's kingship and priesthood. Then, the Church is a community founded upon a common faith, sharing a common hope, an eschatological expectation, and living by the Spirit the life of love which is God the Father's love for the Son and therefore for the Church. Finally, the Church, like any other institution persisting through time, articulates and makes possible its common life through an internal ordering according to which particular groups of men are charged with particular functions; and, since the community is pressed from time to time to formulate for itself what its common beliefs are, among the offices and functions we find what is called in Latin theology the *magisterium*, a teaching with authority, an authority which, naturally, is not derived from the Church considered as an independently existing historical

institution but from the authority of Christ sacramentally identified with his Church. It also belongs to the
historical reality of the Church that this, as it were,
interior dialogue of the Church with itself, through
which it learns ever more about the message which the
Lord has committed to it, is a necessary part of its life.
Theology, that is, reflection upon the Church's understanding of itself, is not something that might not have
been and need not be. (Here it differs from dogmatic
definition which may be thought equally a necessity of
the Church's life, but a sad necessity.[10]) At the same
time, it also belongs to the historical reality of the Church
that what is taught by the *magisterium* is taught in and
through the forms of thought and the language of particular periods. It is a necessary part of the concept of
incarnation that incarnation should be in particular
places and at particular times. Once again, and not
accidentally, the balance of orthodoxy here strictly
parallels the balance of orthodoxy in Christology. The
balance is kept by resisting two impulses: one, to
absolutize the forms of thought and expressions of particular periods, to fail to see the *historical* character of
what the Church utters at a given time; the other, to
dissolve away the sense of the dogmatic teaching, so
that in the end we are left simply with an inexpressible
something hard to distinguish from nothing. Bultmann
and Tillich are examples of the latter tendency, some
scholastic (in spirit Cartesian) theologians of the former.

In the apostolic and sub-apostolic Church priesthood
is ascribed only to Christ (as in Hebrews) and to the
Church as the people of God: the new Israel is a priestly

people, as was the old Israel (cf. I Peter 2. 4-10). There is in fact only one priesthood, one mediator between God and man, one only who offers the sacrifice of himself to God and declares the Torah of the new Covenant. The Church is priestly in virtue of its identification with and participation in the priesthood of Christ. The bishops who take care of the churches and the presbyters who share their ministerial and pastoral functions are never at this period called priests, *sacerdotes*. Thus, in so far as there is a *sacerdotium* in the early Church, it is not one which is thought of as being independent of Christ's priesthood and of that priesthood which all Christians enter upon through baptism and the gift of the Spirit. This restriction of the application of priesthood to Christ and to the Christian community had a certain polemical purpose in that the early Christians wished to distinguish themselves from Judaism, in which there was a priestly caste, and from the notions of priesthood common in the pagan cults that forced themselves upon their attention in the great cities of the Empire.

By the third century, it had become commonplace to speak of the bishop as the high priest, as the man in the community who enjoys the fullness of the priesthood and gives to his presbyters a share in his office and work.[11] This has been interpreted by some Protestant theologians[12] as a falling away from the integrity of the apostolic period, an addition, through syncretism, to the apostolic preaching. Even if it were true that as a matter of history syncretism was here at work, as it certainly was by this time in the fields of liturgy and organization, the theology of the matter offers no difficulty. The priestly activity of the community comes to a focus in the eucharistic assembly and sacrificial meal. This is the sacrament of Christ's sacrifice to the Father. Over this assembly the bishop presides, as guardian of the apostolic witness, so that it can even be said that where the bishop is, there is the Church, and also as the minister of the eucharistic mystery, the one who "offers" it, as Christ continually presents the same sacrifice in the heavenly places. He, in union with all the baptized, does sacramentally what Christ does and thus participates in a special way in the priestly activity of Christ. This participation is not exclusive, except in its mode; it in no way contradicts the fundamental dogma that through baptism all the faithful are sharers in Christ's priesthood, as in all his other functions and acts. But it belongs to the nature of the Church as a society, and above all a society that finds its religious centre in the eucharistic assembly, that there is a diversity of functions in which the guardianship of the apostolic witness and ministerial priestly activity are both concentrated in the person of the bishop. It is not of course claimed that there is or could be an *a priori* proof that this is how the common life of the Church had to be articulated; but that this is how it was articulated; and that there are no historical or theological grounds for supposing that this development represents a falling away from primitive integrity.

That there is nevertheless a falling away, one which reached a climax in the Middle Ages and still deforms the theological thinking of the West, in another, related sphere, is plain. This falling away shows itself in two ways: in the understanding of the role of the ministerial priesthood (especially that aspect of its role which is concerned with authority within and "over" the Church); and in the understanding of the relationship between the Church and the political authorities.

Where the common life of a society is articulated through a variety of offices linked with functions, it is necessary that some offices and functions should seem to be and should really be more important than others. If, as I have argued, the ministerial priesthood of the bishop is an essential and divinely willed office in the Church, still more if it is true that the office of the successor of Peter is divinely willed, then there is a sense in which these offices are essential to the being and not simply to the well-being, of the Church. This distinction between the bishop and the rest of the faithful exists for the sake of the faithful; the sacrament of order exists for the sake of the community and has no other *raison d'être*. But since the actual condition of men in the Church is that of men who are *en route* but have not yet arrived, a condition in which sin is a possibility and in which the psychological deformations that go with every kind of specialized work are also possibilities, it would be strange if there were not in the day-to-day life of the Church, existing as it has done under very difficult and painful historical conditions, much which fails to correspond to the image of authentic authority offered by Christ himself. Out of many possible examples I choose, as bringing out the most striking features of this image, a part of Christ's discourse which is placed by Luke immediately after the last supper and just before the agony in the garden. This placing of the discourse emphasizes the supreme didactic significance attached to it by the primitive Christian community out of which Luke's narrative comes.

A dispute arose among them, which of them was to be regarded as the greatest. And he said to them, "The kings of the Gentiles exercise lordship over them; and those in authority over them are called benefactors. But not so with you; rather let the greatest among you become as the youngest, and the leader as one who serves. For which is the greater, one who sits at table, or one who serves? Is it not the one who sits at table? But I am among you as one who serves" (Luke 22. 24-27).

Authority, then, is a service of the brethren; and the one who exercises supreme authority in the Christian community is the servant of all. In the age of the Fathers this principle of authority is directly expressed in the institutional patterns of the community. Bishops are elected by the clergy and the laity, and decisions are made in consultation with the whole Christian people. Cyprian tells us how he views his exercise of the episcopal office: "I have made it a rule, ever since the beginning of my episcopate, to make no decision merely on the strength of my own personal opinion without consulting you [the priests and the deacons], without the approbation of the people."[13] One of the most ancient of the papal titles is *servus servorum Dei*. It is impossible to deny that this pattern grows weaker and in the end changes, until it becomes a mere theory unrelated to common practice. Men come to think of the *sacerdotium* as no longer an office of service within the Church but as a power exercised over the Church. More, the very term *ecclesia* which in Scripture, in the Liturgy, and in the writings of the Fathers means the whole people of God is appropriated to the *sacerdotium*, narrowly conceived, and even to the curial government of the Church in Rome. The older and more authentic tradition is never wholly lost, for the daily food of the reflective theologian and the spontaneously evinced pattern of Christian sanctity are too scriptural, too liturgical, too patristic, for the tradition ever to fall quite out of sight.

All this is much more than a matter merely of sin and professional deformation. The collapse of European society in the Dark Ages and the implication of the Church in the feudal system, the alliance between throne and altar which was the legacy of the Reformation and Counter-Reformation in Europe, all these and other factors are of immense importance in this development. It is with the final disintegration of these hierarchical social structures in modern times that it has been possible to perceive the original brightness of the evangelical principle of authority. This was very clear to John XXIII, who, in the place where spiritual authority had been most confused with lordship as the kings of the Gentiles understand it, began the deep process of reform which will in the end produce a more adequate reflection of what ecclesiastical authority essentially is in the institutional structure of the Christian community. The faithful are beginning to free themselves from a kind of ecclesiastical myth. This has been well described by Schillebeeckx:

> Many of the faithful have a kind of totalitarian notion of the Church, and confuse the absolute claims of a Church in which the Hierarchy does hold the office of administration of Christ's visible grace with a sort of secular dictatorial power arrogated to itself by the Church, and making of the laity nothing more than a group of subjects who can carry out only what the Hierarchy decides they must do. This notion is not only incorrect; it is completely alien to the true character of the Church and is in fact heretical.[14]

When, from the Flaminian Gate, Cardinal Wiseman proclaimed the restoration of the Catholic hierarchy in England, it was for the Protestant imagination of England as though the ghost of Pius V, bearing a copy of the Bull, *Regnans in excelsis*, had taken a living substance. Of course, this was mostly a contrived political melodrama not to be taken more seriously than the warnings that accompanied the campaign against the late Al Smith when he ran for the presidency of the United States. All the same, the melodrama presupposed a persisting picture of the relations between Church and State that was no farther from the actualities of history than an apt caricature is from its original. The spirit of the medieval papacy, by no means an ignoble spirit and one which witnessed to the spiritual life in a brutal age, is in political matters represented by Innocent III, who wrote to the Archbishop of Ravenna: "The liberty of the Church is

81

nowhere better served than where the Roman Church obtains full power both in temporal and in spiritual matters."[15] When one thinks of the princes of Europe at that time, one sees why he takes this view. But the exercise of both the direct and the indirect power by the Church was in the end a monumental failure, inevitable as it may have been in the circumstances of the period, and motivated as it was, from the time of the Hildebrandine reforms, by a determination to free the Church from the limitations imposed by feudalism and the territorial church system. It was broken against the more powerful forces of secularism and nationalism, forces it had done something to nourish and provoke.

This whole period, from the eleventh to the fifteenth century, is the most fascinating of all periods to the theorist of law and politics, and many of its most fundamental questions of interpretation are still open. But over one thing there is no doubt: it was the Imperialists and Regalists rather than the Canonists, Marsilius rather than Aquinas, who gave modern political thought its characteristic themes and spirit. This has the curious result that the Church came out of the Middle Ages tied to a political ambition that only the most visionary could think it possible to entertain. This ambition was not, except for very brief periods and in relation to peculiar situations, one which yearned for the exercise of direct political power. The yearning was rather for that type of alliance with the political authorities in which these authorities would be the secular arm of the spiritual, maintaining religious orthodoxy among their subjects and deferring to the Church where, in the

Church's judgment, moral or religious issues were in question. Even when it became clear that the only party to profit by this arrangement was the political authority rather than the Church, that to exact services of this kind from the political authority was to make this authority in effect the guardian of orthodoxy and thus to enslave the Church (one thinks of Philip II of Spain and his use of the Inquisition, and of the whole history of Gallicanism), so that more and more the ecclesiastical settlement in the Catholic countries came to resemble the settlement in those Protestant countries—northern Germany, Scandinavia, England—where out of the Reformation came State Churches with monarchs of a caesaro-papistical kind at their heads;[16] even then, and after the Church had accommodated itself to the societies that followed the collapse of the Old Regime, there was still a persistent belief that somehow a state of affairs in which the powers of the political authority were at the disposal of the Church and in which heresy was banished and orthodoxy maintained by force was the Christian and Catholic ideal. Anything less than this was held to be a temporary accommodation to a decadent world. That such an "ideal" could never have been realized has for long been clear. That it could not intelligibly be said to be a Christian ideal I will try to show.

In its origins this attitude is not medieval. It is a part of the medieval inheritance from the ancient world and goes back to the momentous edict promulgated in A.D. 380, the edict which contains the definition of the Catholic Church already cited (p. 27). The crucial words are:

We order those who follow [the apostolic] doctrine
to receive the title of Catholic Christians, but others
we judge to be mad and raving and worthy of incur-
ring the disgrace of heretical teaching, nor are their
assemblies to receive the name of churches. They are
to be punished not only by Divine retribution but
also by our own measures which we have decided in
accordance with Divine inspiration.[17]

There is no logical gap between this edict of the Theodosian Code and the relation between the Church and
the political authorities presupposed by Aquinas in his
account of the duties of Church and State in relation to
heresy. Of the pertinacious heretic he writes that "the
Church, despairing of his conversion, makes provision
for the safety of others and, having cut him off from
the Church by excommunication, relinquishes him to
the judgment of the secular arm to be eliminated from
the world by death" (*S.Th.* IIa IIae Q.11 a.3). Early Protestantism professed precisely the same doctrine: "In
1546, in answer to the Pope's invitation to the Council
of Trent, Bullinger indignantly repudiates the insinua-
tion that the Protestant cantons were heretical, 'for, by
the grace of God, we have always punished the vices of
heresy and sodomy with fire, and have looked upon
them, and still look upon them, with horror'."[18]
We must now inquire if the data of revelation permit
us to conclude that the relation between Church and
State established by the Theodosian Code and exemplified
in the practice of the Middle Ages and, it should be
added, by Catholic and Protestant practice for long after

the Reformation and Counter-Reformation, is capable of being justified. This is a very different sort of enterprise from an inquiry concerning the sacraments or the sacred ministry. Clearly, a political theory as such or a theory as to the right relation between Church and State cannot be a part of the substance of revelation. Questions of this kind are too closely related to the contingencies of history. One of the crucial texts in this field, that dealing with the lawfulness of paying tribute to Caesar (Matthew 22. 15-22; Mark 12. 13-17; Luke 20. 20-26), is in itself very intimately connected with a political and social order that has passed away. The conditions of living under Tiberius and during President Johnson's Administration are very different, and the concrete duties of the Christian under the one may be different from what they are under the other. At most we shall be able to disengage from the political context within which the apostles preached certain general principles capable of being applied in a variety of political situations.

We have already seen that for the thought of the New Testament the present age was an interim period between the resurrection of Jesus and his return in glory. Christ had already triumphed; the prince of this world was already judged; the principalities and powers that stand behind the forces of nature and society were already subject to him. Nevertheless, the process of reconciling man with God takes place, for the individual and the community, within history and therefore within those institutions that belong to the present age. This is why Paul says that "the governing authorities . . . have been

instituted by God" and have the function of doing retributive justice, and in so doing act as the servants of God,
and have the right to be paid for what they do (Romans
13. 1-7). What belongs to the social nature of man in
the order of creation and also what belongs to the social
nature of man in a world in which the definitive victory
over sin is not yet visibly established are willed by God.
The Christian, therefore, cannot take up an antinomian
position in relation to the State and its ordinances. At
the same time, the doctrine of Paul in this matter cannot
rightly be used as an argument for unconditional obedience. With the passage just quoted we have to link his
rebuke (in I Corinthians 6. 1-8) of those who bring disputes between Christians before the public courts. The
justice of the State, something willed by God, has no
place in the dealings of Christians with each other, for
between Christians the law of retributive justice has
been replaced by the law of love.

The nucleus of the Church's life is thus something
with which the political authorities have no concern;
and these authorities go beyond their divinely authorized
role if they reach out into the inner life of the Church
and command the individual believer to confess that
Caesar is god or that Jesus Christ is accursed. Further,
within the order established by Christ's victory (though
this order, it is important to emphasize, is sacramental
and only as such a historical reality), there is a reversal
of roles in the relation between the Church and the
political authorities. In the passage in which Paul rebukes
the Corinthians for bringing their disputes before the
public courts he asks them why they are incapable of

settling their own disputes; for, as the elect of God, they are to judge the world and "the angels", that is, the *exousiai* or demonic powers that stand behind the State. (But this judgment belongs to eschatology and not to the process of history.) There is thus no conflict between the Pauline teaching and the indictment, by the author of the Apocalypse, of the Roman Empire, depicted under the figure of the great beast that comes out of the sea (Revelation 13. 1-10). For the *exousiai*, the powers and authorities of Romans 13 are the legitimate powers of the political order in so far as they do the work ordained for them by God; in the Apocalypse of John these same powers are seen as perverted by their determination to take the place of God, a determination illustrated by the cult of the divine Caesar which was to serve as a pretext for the persecution of the Church.

The evidence of the Gospels does not conflict with the pastoral teaching of Paul. The mission and preaching of Jesus are fulfilled in his death at the hands of the Roman state. The injustice of the execution is that he was executed as one who sought to establish, through rebellion against the Roman administration, a Jewish theocracy with himself as king. The tragic irony of this lies in his having quite deliberately refused this role. This is shown, not only by the reply he gives when he is questioned about the lawfulness of paying the Roman tribute (the question is an attempt to get him to convict himself either as a Zealot or as a collaborator and thus a traitor to his own nation), but also by the story of the temptation in the wilderness according to which dominion over "the kingdoms of the world" is among the diabolical suggestions he refuses to entertain (Matthew 4. 8-11; Luke 4. 5-8). He does not condemn the State. It is a part of the fabric of the present age and is to be neither divinized nor repudiated. His followers, up to the eve of the crucifixion itself, cannot understand fully that the Messianic kingdom is not to be a Jewish theocracy. Cullmann suggests, plausibly, that the reluctance of Jesus to refer directly to his Messianic role in public springs from the inevitability with which this would have been taken as a theocratic claim.[19] The community founded upon Peter's confession is not to be a political state. This would be radically incompatible with the preaching of the good news of the coming of God's kingdom; and the political order is something provisional, whereas the *ecclesia* is the sign of the new world order that will be revealed in glory at the end of the present age.

We may collect from this short consideration of the New Testament evidence the following principles: The State is willed by God and is thus a part of the order of creation; but if we think of its distinctive function as being the administration of retributive justice—and this is the function Paul picks out—then there is a sense in which this is a necessary part of the State only in relation to man's actual situation, that of being a sinner. Man as redeemed, in the fellowship of the Church, can dispense with this principle, not as a citizen but as a Christian. The belief that the State is willed by God corresponds to the view that it exists "by nature"; that its distinctive function should be penal springs from human sin, so that the State is indeed *poena et remedium peccati*, and in this sense it exists "by convention". But it cannot be inferred from the New Testament that this latter is all that the State is.

It is the characteristic temptation suffered by the followers of Jesus to understand the Messianic kingdom, signified by the Church, as a kingdom which gathers to itself all powers. This is to confuse the Church with the *regnum Christi*. All power is indeed possessed by Christ, but he wills the actualization of the redemption within history through the Church, and this has a law and a being quite other than those of the State and exists over against the State. State absolutism is satanic; but so, too, is theocracy, open or disguised; and so, too, is the doctrine that the distinctive activity of the Church, the works of love, should be safeguarded by the powers of the State.

If it is correct to say that the State is willed by God and is thus a part of the order of creation—however much its actual functions may be conditioned by human sin—does it follow that one of the criteria for recognizing what is truly a state and distinguishing it from a pseudo-state will be that a true state acknowledges itself as being under God's rule? This cannot be so from the standpoint of the New Testament, for the state about which Paul speaks in the Letter to the Romans, the state which the Lord himself refers to when he tells inquirers to give to Caesar what belongs to Caesar, this state is given over to idolatry and is thus incapable of ascribing to itself that role it occupies in the order established by God. (That it is given over to idolatry is later to be stressed by Augustine as the mark of the essential injustice of the Roman state; but this is in a highly polemical context.) Even a state, then, which has a perverted

89

understanding of its role and function nevertheless has that role and performs that function assigned to it by God. At the same time, it is the characteristic tendency of this state—though not only of this pagan state—to turn itself into a pseudo-theocracy. This is indeed the standard pattern of the State in the ancient world, and not even the (in one sense) very secular democratic cities of the Greeks escaped this characteristic perversion, as the indictment of Socrates shows. Even this is not a sufficient condition for the Christian to withdraw his allegiance, for the Roman state in the period of the New Testament is such a pseudo-theocracy.

What, then, if anything, marks the distinction between that state Paul says we should obey and the great beast, the tool of Satan, depicted by the author of the Apocalypse? I believe it is impossible to answer this question simply, to say that such and such is the point beyond which the state to which we owe obedience is transformed into the state we are morally obliged to resist. Even the worst state can scarcely avoid doing much that has to be done if human life is to be possible. Obedience to the State is in respect of this or that sort of conduct it requires of us; so that even in a very bad state it cannot be true that everything the State forbids is allowed and everything the State enjoins is to be resisted. The State may command us to serve in an unjust war or to take part in idolatrous worship, and here, naturally, the State must be resisted; but it may also require us to observe our contracts or to vaccinate our children, and here it must be obeyed. The mark of the supremely unjust state, and in the sense of the Apocalypse this will be the mark

of the beast, is the attempt to impose idolatry, to pene-
trate into the intimate life of the Church and usurp the
authority of the Lord of the Church. This is the mark
of the beast and it is this that the totalitarian states of
our period have exemplified most clearly; though we
deceive ourselves if we think that political freedom in
itself is a guarantee that this cannot happen in states of
another kind. In the categories of thought of the New
Testament writers, this is where the demonic powers
attempt to assert their independence of Christ's authority; and the witness of the martyrs is the human sign,
and the *only* such sign, that, all appearances to the contrary notwithstanding, Christ reigns. That Christ should
be seen to reign, not in earthly splendour, but in the
broken bodies of the martyrs, in Auschwitz or Karaganda,
as once in the circuses of the ancient world, this is the
sign of that *peripeteia*, reversal of roles, so much stressed
in the Gospels. That Nero, Stalin, Hitler, Verwoerd, the
present rulers in Mississippi or Alabama should all of
them co-exist with the *regnum Christi* is a severe trial
of faith, and the witness of the martyrs which preserves
the faith of those who are not required to be witnesses
to the point of death—we are all called to this degree
of witness but it is not required of all—is the witness of
men whose faith triumphs despite the appearance of the
triumph of evil. So Cyprian witnessed to the faith "under
the Emperors Valerian and Gallienus, but in the reign of
our Lord Jesus Christ, to whom is honour and glory for
ever and ever." And so, we may add, did James Chaney,
Andrew Goodman, and Michael Schwerner in the State
of Mississippi in the year of our Salvation 1964.[20]

IV

The Secular Society

So far we have emphasized the eschatological in Christian faith. The Christian lives under the great signs, mysteries or sacraments, which effectively realize for the community and the individual believer the mighty acts in which God has visited and redeemed his people. I have argued that it is an implication of this idea of Christian faith that all powers belong to the *regnum Christi*; that the Church, as a community with an articulated, divinely willed structure, is the principal sign of the *regnum Christi*; that the role of the State is divinely willed; that the State as an institution is a part of the order of creation and belongs to the integrity of human nature—however much its distinctive features derive their characteristic modes of operation from the sinfulness of the human family; and that the characteristic perversion of both the Church and the State is theocracy: an attempt by the Church to gather to itself all powers; an attempt by the State to make of itself an absolute authority requiring of its subjects religious obedience. This eschatological emphasis has been a necessary part of the enterprise of asking what the apostolic witness was in these matters.

Now, it may be observed that it is no longer possible for the Christian believer to feel the pressure of the *eschaton*, the end, in precisely the way the men of the apostolic period did. Granted that it is central to Christian faith that we look to the life of the age to come, the consummation of human history, it is all the same true that Christianity and secular culture have gone through a long and complex historical development and that our whole conception of human history and cosmic change is something quite outside the thought of a man of the ancient world or of the Middle Ages. New tasks, new problems, impose themselves on the Christian thinker. The absolute seriousness and relevance, for our own as for every epoch, of the apostolic witness is not in question; but the concrete situations that confront us are not those that confronted Paul or Aquinas or Luther or Ignatius Loyola; and these new situations are what they are in part because human history has been penetrated by Christian faith, so that it is no longer possible to look at the phenomena of secular history without putting the question: How far is what we find there a Christian work and responsibility?

It is important to notice that we "put the question". For here we come upon something deeply problematical. There can be no question of proofs or demonstrations. To take an example, one may put the question: Why did natural science in the form it took from Galileo onwards develop in Europe and not in the—in many respects—more sophisticated civilization of China? I do not think there can be a conclusive answer to such a question as this, no matter how rich the historical material at our disposal may be. It is a question of a quite different order from a question about the historical origin of the clock or the compass. Such a question can in principle be settled. We can certainly state a number of necessary conditions for the emergence of natural science, among them the inheritance of Greek philosophy and the mathematical techniques developed by the Arabs. Again, it is impossible to conceive the work of Galileo or Kepler apart from a certain stage of technical development in the grinding of lenses for telescopes. One could greatly extend the list of necessary conditions. But if one were to ask for a sufficient condition or for a proof that a given set of necessary conditions was taken as a whole sufficient, it is not clear what kind of answer would in principle be satisfactory. This is not to say that all speculation in this field is idle. It is to say that the categories of thought in terms of which we expect a speculative answer are essentially disputable; and this is so because the subject matter of the speculation is human history; and human history appears to be a field qualitatively distinct from the field studied by the natural scientist. In human history, the idea of "sufficient condition" is not a clear one; and the reason for this is, very roughly, that the concepts of freedom and creation have an application in the field of human history.

Given all these cautions and provisos, is there anything a Christian can plausibly say about the phenomena of secular history considered as in part a Christian work and responsibility?

There are in the first place what we may reasonably take to be some of the distinctive achievements of the Middle Ages. In the very little we have so far said about medieval culture it has been the negative or dark side that has been stressed, and this simply because we have been concerned with strictly ecclesiastical questions and not with the wider questions about the penetration of human culture by Christianity. Here the picture of the Middle Ages must be quite different, for it is in the Middle Ages proper and not during the ambiguous period of the Renaissance that the world we now inhabit is given its characteristic structures of thought and its characteristic themes.

It seems evident, for example, that constitutional government and the rule of law are medieval inventions, not in the sense that these ideas are totally unknown to Greek or (for all I know) to Indian or Chinese speculation, but in the sense that these ideas are in the medieval period operative, genuine determinants of policy, and are shown in the modern period to have a certain capacity to endure. I do not think that in this field the broad conclusions of an older generation of historians and political philosophers, Acton, Figgis, the Carlyles, Maitland, to mention only scholars writing in English, have been shaken by recent work, however much they may have been shown to be wrong on particular points. Acton's account seems hard to challenge.

Representative government, which was unknown to the ancients, was almost universal. The methods of election were crude; but the principle that no tax was lawful that was not granted by the class that paid it —that is, that taxation was inseparable from representation—was recognized, not as the privilege of certain countries, but as the right of all. Not a prince in the world, said Philip de Commines, can levy a penny without the consent of the people. Slavery was almost everywhere extinct; and absolute power was deemed more intolerable and more criminal than slavery. The right of insurrection was not only admitted but defined, as a duty sanctioned by religion. Even the principles of the Habeas Corpus Act, and the method of the income tax, were already known. The issue of ancient politics was an absolute state planted on slavery. The political produce [*sic*] of the Middle Ages was a system of states in which authority was restricted by the representation of powerful classes, by privileged associations, and by the acknowledgment of duties superior to those which are imposed by man. As regards the realization in practice of what was seen to be good, there was almost everything to do. But the great problems of principle had been solved.[1]

Of course, an explanation of some of this which disregards the contribution of Christianity to the shaping of medieval culture is perfectly possible. Acton himself suggests that the growth of civil liberty can be understood as a consequence of the collision between the political and the ecclesiastical authorities, "the aim of both contending parties [being] absolute authority".[2] But if we place the political developments within the broader context of medieval culture, it may be argued that within a culture penetrated by the anthropology of the Christian faith, by a certain conception of God and of the relation between God and the world, and by the belief that spiritual authority transcends all social structures and their requirements, much was possible, in politics as in other spheres, that would not otherwise have been possible.

I choose two features of this context as especially significant: the reception of Aristotelianism; and the appearance of Franciscan spirituality. These can be treated as two aspects of a single process, the appearance in a new form of ancient themes, fundamentally biblical, that had been overshadowed by the influence of Neo-Platonism, through Augustine and the Pseudo-Denys and Boethius, on early medieval theology. In both the reality of sensible objects is affirmed as against all Platonizing. Both are empiricist, seeking God in and through creatures. *Nihil est in intellectu quod non prius fuerit in sensu* ("There is nothing in the intellect which is not first in the senses"), said the Aristotelian schoolman. There is here no doubt about the robustness of his empiricism. Equally, Franciscan spirituality celebrates in a perfectly naturalistic way the material world. This celebration is in the vernacular, not in Latin, the language of learned men and clerks, and it is a celebration of the simplicity and beauty and, so to speak, companionship of God's creatures: sun, moon, wind, cloud, fire, earth, fruit, and flowers. This is one of the great moments in human history; for the nature celebrated in Francis' "Canticle of the Creatures" is nature freed from the demonic, cleansed of its occult and fearful powers, fresh from the hand of God. This victory over animism is not consolidated before the rise of natural science in the seventeenth century; but it seems likely that this way of approach to nature is as much a precondition of the possibility of natural science as that pervasive rationalism of medieval theology to which Alfred North Whitehead attached so much importance.[3]

D

Both the reception of Aristotle and the spirituality of the Franciscan movement can properly be understood as parts of a vast process of secularization, and one which was impeded rather than furthered by the conflicts of the Reformation period. Both movements are connected with the new religious organizations of the friars, Dominicans and Franciscans; and the growth of the friars is one aspect of the growth of town life, with all that it meant in terms of the strong development of self-governing institutions and of that lay spirit that in so many medieval cities erected the church of Our Lady over against the older romanesque church of the monks. Indeed, at this moment it begins to be clear that in one sense Christianity is at war with *religion*. Though the reception of Christianity normally presupposes—or has hitherto presupposed—the religious consciousness, Christianity under one aspect is not a species of the genus religion, but another genus: the initiative of God in the person of Jesus "who reflects the glory of God and bears the very stamp of his nature", not man's response to the tremendous and fascinating mystery of the nature in which he is immersed and of which he forms a part.

The process of secularization is the cleansing of human culture by the spirit of Christ; and it is also a process in which certain intellectual distinctions are made clearly for the first time. The fundamental distinction is that made by Aquinas between philosophy as an autonomous discipline and theology as the science which takes what has been revealed as its datum. This foreshadows the emancipation of all the positive sciences. Its deep significance for the Christian thinker is not even now fully grasped. Further, moral and political life are also autonomous, since in principle each man in his moral thinking is able to share in the Divine reason; and the distinction between Church and State, *sacerdotium* and *regnum*, rests upon a distinction of function which is respected by the best medieval thinkers, however much it is blurred in the course of the conflicts between the Papacy and the Empire or the Papacy and the French Crown.

European history is often represented schematically as a transition from a culture shaped by religion to an opposing secular culture, that culture within which we now live. There is a certain crude truth in this, more especially if we think of how a culture represents itself for the imagination, through the arts. But I wish to maintain that secularization is the work of a spiritual impulse that comes from Christian faith and is a consequence of what is implicit in the outlook of the Bible and the apostolic preaching.[4] To use the forms of thought of the New Testament, the principalities and powers are now subjected to Christ. Everything belongs to him and thus the distinction between the secular and the sacred is something with only provisional validity. The possibility of tragedy and retrogression is not excluded, for the burden of freedom can always be refused. We can always fall back upon the comforts of idolatry and we can even transform the worship of the true God into an idolatrous cult. But the forms of idolatry that belong to the modern period are more plainly tricks played by man upon himself, forms of self-alienation, to use the Hegelian-Marxist terminology. For Marx, all religion is the product of human alienation; man sees the work of his own consciousness as something existing over against him and having the spurious vitality of a fetish. This is indeed true of idolatry, as Paul points out.

> Ever since the creation of the world his invisible nature, namely, his eternal power and deity, has been clearly perceived in the things that have been made. So [the Gentiles] are without excuse; for although they knew God they did not honour him as God or give thanks to him, but they became futile in their thinking and their senseless minds were darkened. Claiming to be wise, they became fools, and exchanged the glory of the immortal God for images resembling mortal man or birds or animals or reptiles (Romans 1. 20-23).

The work of human alienation is subtler in the modern period, for men are no longer disposed to divinize men or the brutes in the simple pagan way; but the "Supreme Being" of the Deists, a kind of honorary President of a mechanical universe, the Hegelian Absolute, the historical dialectic, are only more sophisticated, not less idolatrous. Once men have known the true God their idolatries mimic truth more closely. The synthetic deities just mentioned are all of them formally derived from the idea of the God who is the Lord of the Universe and of human history; and the most potent myth of the modern age, Marxism, contrives to mimic the very pattern of redemption. Man falls away from the integrity of primitive communism, suffers in the fallen world of class society, is redeemed by the most suffering class of modern society, the proletariat, achieving salvation through the final struggle of this class with the powers of darkness, and finding on the far side of the proletarian revolution a reintegrated and glorified humanity, the kingdom of freedom in place of the kingdom of necessity.

Secularization, then, is not a negative process. The great temptation for the Christian is to suppose that it can be reversed and that Christianity can once more mould human society in such a way that the form and content of culture are overtly and explicitly Christian. This cannot happen precisely because the Christian energies have broken and dissolved the religious pattern of culture that marked off both the ancient and the early medieval worlds. At the same time, secularism can be turned into a religion, as it was in France from the Revolution to the Third Republic;[5] or a vague Christian religiosity can sanctify the *mores* of a fundamentally secular society.[6] This last possibility is perhaps the most dangerous of all, just because it may appear so beguiling. The spirit of paganism is then located outside the society in question, just as much—and with less excuse—as it was by the sacral society of the Middle Ages. Communism, for example, is always *atheistic* communism for the propagandists of social conservatism, as though for all the world they were gripped by *odium theologicum*. But the sanctification of the *mores* of a secular society by Christian religiosity is as much an attempt to construct a pseudo-theocracy as the more obvious and more obviously repulsive attempt by a totalitarian regime to demand of men the obedience that can be given only to God. The cleansing of the sensibility and the clarification of the intellect, with all that has accompanied these in the way of greater humanity and tolerance, are not therefore the fruits of an inevitably beneficent process. Secularization offers greater possibilities for Christian faith because this faith is no longer tied to primitive forms of thought and to indefensible political attitudes; but the secular society sets its own traps for the Christian, most of all the trap constituted by the belief that at bottom Christianity and "the values of the national community", or "the tradition of the West", or "the precious heritage of western man", or some other delusive formula, are pretty much the same thing.[7]

We have already seen that if the State exists "by nature" and as such belongs to what man is in creation, it does not follow that the State must so acknowledge itself. This is clear enough in the Pauline teaching about the Roman state. The role of the State is realized in what it does, not in what it declares itself to be; and there is even a danger that a state too conscious of its divinely willed character and not enough aware that whatever in human affairs is willed by God is also under the judgment of God will attempt to turn itself into a bad theocracy and claim what belongs to God alone. No modern state of the "western" democratic type makes such a claim today, nor does it on the other hand in any formal way admit that its authority is vicarious. But it is a mistake to suppose that the modern doctrine of sovereignty is a formal denial of the principle that the State's authority is vicarious. I have already argued that the doctrine of sovereignty is either a doctrine about what is logically required for a complete and consistent system of law or it is the view, scarcely controvertible, that it is a defining characteristic of a state as distinct from a municipal authority that its laws are not subject to scrutiny or control by any higher authority; but here the expression "any higher authority" refers only to a secular legal authority and not to the authority of God or the moral law. God and the moral law are, on the whole, carefully excluded from the courts as being outside their competence. But it is all the same commonly held in democratic societies that an authority which is undoubtedly sovereign may at the same time be illegitimate, and thus not the source of morally binding commands.

There was no doubt where, in terms of positive, enforceable law, sovereignty lay in the greater German Reich ruled by Hitler at the height of his power; but it would have been curious in the extreme to suppose that the commands of the Reich, commands of unimpeachable validity from a purely legal standpoint, laid even a trifling moral obligation upon an inhabitant of the General Government or of conquered Bohemia. It would be equally curious to suppose that the racial legislation of the Third Reich imposed moral obligations upon German citizens; and yet there can be no doubt that the Nuremberg Laws were good law by all the Austinian or Hobbesian criteria. Almost the only satisfaction to be derived from the otherwise unsatisfactory trial of the major war criminals at Nuremberg was that it committed the Allied Powers to the principle that there may be circumstances in which a man is bound to resist the lawful commands of his lawful superiors and that a man who does not so resist may be punished notwithstanding his plea that what he did he was required to do by positive law. No more than this is required for it to be possible to apply the concept of vicarious authority to the modern state. On the one hand, there is an identifiable source of power; on the other, there is the judgment of the individual citizen *in foro interno*, a judgment which is both a declaration of and a submission to that which lies beyond all positive law and all concrete political institutions.

It is a commonplace that the modern state has a more positive social role than any earlier type of state. The fundamental reason for this is that the economic life of modern society is so dynamic and so potentially destructive of the fortunes of individuals and groups that to leave all our social activities to be determined by the device of the free market would be both inhumane and politically disastrous. If we are to avoid social cannibalism and gross economic instability we have to see to it that the public authorities are powerful and technically expert. One aspect of the positive role of the modern state is its activity in the field of education. It is here that the *regnum* and the *sacerdotium* are in our society most likely to clash; and I should like to examine some of the principles involved in this delicate field.

Christian bodies have been pioneers of public education at every level, from the elementary school to the university, that invention of the Christian Middle Ages. It is only with the middle-class revolution and the growth of industrialism that public authorities everywhere begin to move into this field; and now they are everywhere predominant, both because they command resources far greater than any at the disposal of other bodies and because in the natural sciences, the technologies, and perhaps already in the social sciences, public authorities have the strongest possible interest in the quality of teaching and research. This latter consideration means that they seek to have an influence even in the private sector of education. In all free societies it is legally possible for private groups to conduct schools, though the State necessarily thinks itself obliged to require and enforce the maintenance of certain minimum standards; and it seems certain, in view of the cost of modern education, that everywhere the private sector will be compelled to retreat, unless, as with the universities in England or with the denominational schools in Scotland or Holland, to pick a few examples out of many, they have the advantage of virtually complete public support without the disadvantage of complete public control.

The attitudes of those bodies that formerly were responsible for a great deal of public education have, with one exception, changed greatly in this century. (The rich, naturally, at least in Great Britain and the United States, hold tenaciously to private education at the grammar-school level, as the prosperity of the preparatory schools in the United States and the oddly named public schools in Great Britain shows.) Broadly speaking, Protestants and Jews have come to accept publicly provided and religiously neutral education. It is the Catholics who maintain schools, colleges, and sometimes universities that are, in terms of organization and, in intention at any rate, in terms of ethos, quite distinct from the schools, colleges, and universities that belong to the public sector. (It will be clear that I have in mind primarily the English-speaking countries and that I am compelled to neglect a variety of special problems. Where, for example, are we to place on the educational chart "private" universities in the United States in those cases where they are still nominally denominational institutions and where, having distinguished departments of scientific research, they are financed on a vast scale out of public funds?)

It can be argued, and there is substance in the argument, that the reason for the special position in which Catholics now find themselves is that popular Protestantism has in the last hundred years changed its fundamental character and is now much less a dogmatic religion than it used to be. The culture of the religiously neutral school is in effect a liberal Protestant culture and is thus naturally acceptable to most Protestants. The liberalizing of Judaism is a parallel phenomenon, and Jews are similarly satisfied with an undogmatic ethical monotheism. A Protestant culture which is so vestigially Christian has little about it to offend the agnostic. Only the Catholics are unhappy. For them dogmatic questions are neither open nor unimportant; and they therefore think themselves obliged by the desire to preserve their religious heritage to organize, so far as they can, an educational system with a strong and distinctive religious foundation. Since their schools serve the community in that they also educate children and young people in the secular subjects and in so doing mitigate the pressure on the public sector, it follows (so the argument runs) that they are entitled in strict justice to be assisted out of the public funds to which the parents of Catholic children make the same contribution as do those parents whose children are educated at the public expense.

This is an argument with a number of premises. One, for Catholics, is crucial: that in a pluralist society, and all free societies are in effect pluralist, it is essential, if not for the being, at least for the well-being of the Church, that an education the content of which is largely secular should be under ecclesiastical control. That such ecclesiastical control is essential for the well-being of the Church —and let us understand by well-being not something trivial, such as the Church's prosperity as an institution among others, but something theologically respectable —this looks like a claim that should in principle be capable of some kind of empirical check; and those who defend this premise very frequently speak as though such a check were possible, as, for example, when they argue that juvenile delinquency, or sexual depravity among adolescents, would be diminished if education were less "godless", with the implication that "godly" education produces conspicuously better results in such matters. And no doubt one could test the extent to which church membership is better maintained among those who have attended parochial and other religious schools than among those who have attended religiously neutral schools, though it might be difficult in so complex a situation to take into account all the variables. There seem to be no conclusive studies in this field; and it seems to be the common view among teachers with experience in both systems that the only factor which enables one to make predictions about future religious practice with any confidence is knowledge of the family background of the child, irrespective of whether the child attends a religious school or not. But I am not satisfied that empirical considerations of this kind are either decisive or, in the last analysis, relevant. If it were the case that the religious schools uniformly produced children and young people who were less troublesome to the public authorities, less disturbing to their elders, and more assiduous in attending public worship, this might only mean that they were effective as conditioning agencies. The witness of the Church, in preaching and in sacramental life, is for the sake of the sanctification of the community and the individual that they may be effectively joined to Christ. Individuals marked by those virtues most esteemed in middle-class society are not necessarily a sign of an effective Christian witness. The economy of grace, even the visible economy of grace which is the sacramental life of the Christian people, is not in the end capable of being analyzed quantitatively. This is not to say that holiness and all the charisms that mark a living Christian community are altogether hidden; but it would be a piece of gross materialism to suppose that they could be estimated quantitatively or to suppose that a flourishing ecclesiastical apparatus is necessarily the sign of a community in which things are going well.

Once again, it may be profitable to inquire what the position of the Church in the early centuries was, in this case what it was *vis-à-vis* the educational system of the ancient world.

It seems clear in these centuries Christian education, that is, education in the Scriptures and the sacred traditions, in moral matters, and in the liturgy, was the business of the Church (this meant that it was in practice under the personal supervision of the bishop) and of the family. Education touched adult persons very closely, for the Church was not recruited for the most part from groups that were traditionally Christian but from those already mature who came to the Church asking for baptism and admission to the mysteries. We have almost forgotten, though there are many traces of it in the liturgy, that membership in the Church was then something to be approached through a long period of preparation and instruction, the catechumenate. The preparation of the catechumens was perhaps the chief educational business of the local churches. This was done outside the liturgy by teachers responsible to the bishop; and within that part of the liturgy open to the catechumens through preaching and through the public reading of the Scriptures. A system of religious education which concentrated upon childhood and adolescence, and virtually ended with adolescence, would have been inconceivable to the men of that period.

In this period Christians everywhere used the literary skills and the forms of thought of Hellenistic culture; and these they acquired in the pagan schools. "Never throughout the whole of antiquity, except for a few particular cases, did the Christians set up their own special schools. They simply added their own specifically religious training—which . . . came from the Church and the family—on to the classical teaching that they received along with their non-Christian fellows in the established schools."[8] And this, it should be noted, was at a time when the missionary effort of the Church was uniquely successful. It seems likely that one of the conditions of success was this free relationship between the Christians and their non-Christian fellows. The Church itself was, to a far greater extent than later, an esoteric society, with neophytes and initiates. Becoming a Christian involved an arduous preparation, and even the catechumens were excluded from the mysteries. But there was no disposition to make this carefully guarded inner life of the Church the central point of a spiritual and cultural ghetto. Contemporary Judaism, with the great institution of the rabbinical school, did tend to create such a ghetto; but in this the Christians were decisively different, being open to the world that they might declare the Torah of the new covenant to the world in which they lived.

Granted all this, we have now to ask if there are today special circumstances which make what was possible in the world of antiquity impossible or undesirable in the modern world. We may note that the classical school was in no way a religiously neutral school. It offered a culture which breathed the spirit of paganism. All that was most beautiful and most beguiling in this culture was connected with the cult of the old gods. The situation today is quite different. At least in the English-speaking countries, the religiously neutral school is still benevolent towards Christianity, however little of its substance it may understand; and the thin gruel of positivism and secularism that may be offered in France or Italy has scarcely the charm of ancient paganism and is unlikely to make converts among even moderately robust Christians. More important, Christian faith has nothing to fear from the serious pursuit of what are now autonomous disciplines: history, the critical study of literature, the natural and the social sciences. On the contrary, the present vigour of these subjects is, we have argued, in part a consequence of the working out of principles that originate with the Christian and biblical view of the world. And Christians have everything to fear from any pursuit of these disciplines where the conclusions sought are prescribed, through timidity or conservatism, from without.

My conclusion, then, is that the considerations in favour of what we have described as one premise of the argument for the preserving of a separate and distinctive system of education for children and adolescents are unconvincing; and that there are some historical grounds for believing that a common school, in which the children of Christians of various kinds together with the children of "pagans" are educated side by side, would be a means of breaking out of what remains of the cultural and spiritual ghetto constructed by and for Catholics since the sixteenth century. (I leave aside the much more difficult question of higher education. While this is more difficult to analyze, its practical significance is less. For despite the complexity of institutions and methods in the university field, the world of the university is clearly *one* world within which there are relations of the utmost freedom. Except in the theological faculties, though even in these the atmosphere is changing swiftly, the canons by which the work of scholars is judged are precisely the same whatever the affiliation of the particular university. Any university which is tempted to employ other and less exacting canons, and equally any university inclined to think religion and theology unsuited to academic study, is in need of self-criticism.)

One might then go on to ask (though emphasizing once again that any judgment on the *religious* significance of an educational institution or method in terms of what can be measured by the ordinary techniques of social inquiry has no final relevance) if in fact the religious school does produce men and and women with a distinctive attitude to life. Does it produce those who are able to transcend, to a greater degree than their fellows, all that is meretricious, trivial, and morally obnoxious in our culture? Can they be recognized as having distinctive and higher standards of thought and action in domestic and international politics? More. Catholicism in the present age has been summoned, by a pope of singular gifts, to an *aggiornamento*, to a meeting with the contemporary world, to a casting-off of medieval and Tridentine garments, to a more vigorous use of those biblical and patristic modes of expression and thought that bring out more clearly what Catholics have in common with their separated brethren. Is it the case that those whose religious culture has been most clearly stamped, in childhood and adolescence, with the mark of the education given in the religious school have been the most apt to understand and to respond to this message? These are rhetorical questions, for the answers are reasonably clear prior to any close sociological examination. Finally, to put an even more plainly rhetorical question, if we believe, with John XXIII, that Christians are in this age called to give themselves to a preaching of the Gospel in the language and in the forms of thought of this century, and to a loving penetration of a world in which there is great good as well as great evil, can we believe that this can be combined with the retention of institutions that attempt, with imperfect success, to isolate children from the common life and the common problems of a free society?

The abandoning of a separate system of education— of course, I do not pronounce on the speed with which this should be done, or the degree of completeness with which it should be done at particular times and in particular places, or whether in certain peculiar circumstances (as, for example, where public education is markedly "ideological") it should be done at all—would compel Christians to reflect more seriously on the educational role that in theory belongs to the family and to the Church of God in particular places. Too often the rights and responsibilities of families are weakened and even eroded by a school system administered in an authoritarian fashion—isn't it notoriously the case that associations of parents and teachers are very often much more vigorous in the public than in the religious sector of education?—and too often the immensely serious work of Christian education, a Christian *paideia* organically related to the Gospel, is drained of its vitality by a concentration of thought and resources upon the maintenance and conduct of the religious school; so that the nonsacramental life of the particular congregation is given over to triviality (or worse), and the sacramental life is imperfectly grasped and is thus not given that response its intrinsic dignity requires. Christian education is concerned with bringing men and women to maturity in their faith, not with the administration of a theologically impoverished culture thought—wrongly —to be suitable for children and adolescents. The greatest task confronting those concerned with Christian education is to establish, for those baptized in infancy, something equivalent to the catechumenate of the early Church.

A remarkable feature of the encyclical letters—those concerned with social and political matters—of the late John XXIII was the great change of emphasis, as compared with the encyclical letters of his immediate predecessors, in the treatment of the topic of private ownership. In *Mater et Magistra* it is argued that private ownership is a right always subordinate to *human* rights and to be justified, or not, with reference to its social consequences. (In *Pacem in terris*, it is barely mentioned in the section on human rights.) Instead, it is emphasized that work for a salary or wages is normal and even desirable. After stressing that today it is through various forms of social insurance that men "can face the future with confidence—the sort of confidence which formerly resulted from their possession of a certain amount of property", the author of the Encyclical wrote:

> The modern trend is for people to aim at proficiency in their trade or profession rather than the acquisition of private property. They think more highly of an income which derives from work and the rights consequent upon work, than of an income which derives from capital and the rights of capital. *And this is as*

it should be. Work, which is the immediate expression of a human personality, must always be rated higher than the possession of external goods which of their very nature are merely instrumental. *This view of work is certainly an indication of the advance that has been made in our civilization.*[9]

If to this we add the recognition (of course, not new) of the lawfulness of public ownership of the means of production, the admission of the need for massive public intervention in the economy, the emphasis on the wider political role of the workers, the rebuke of racialist doctrines, the marking of a distinction between communist doctrine and communist practice, then it becomes clear, as it was not perhaps altogether clear under John's predecessors, that Catholicism (in so far as the papacy at a given time can commit it) has broken decisively with all forms of what might be called "romantic" Catholicism that see an affinity between the Church and the old regime or wish to tie Catholicism, and human freedom, to a relatively primitive economy of peasants and craftsmen. To speak in European terms, it suggests there is nothing wrong with a political standpoint that is "left of centre". A mixed economy in which the State has a preponderant power, through public ownership and control over fiscal policy, and in which the basic needs of citizens are met through a combination of professional earnings and social insurance, is a foundation for a good society, though not for a utopia.

This attitude of freedom and acceptance in relation to the social and economic institutions that are beginning to be normal in all the western societies is as reasonable as it is—set against recent history—remarkable. If to this we add the change in theological emphasis that has marked the debates and decrees of the Second Vatican Council, with all that they foreshadow in the way of further changes, then we do not exaggerate in calling this whole set of developments the most important intellectual change of our period (in the field of religion). The process of secularization has reached its term, not with the extinction of Catholic Christianity, not with the dwindling of Catholicism to a social fossil (the lamaism, as it were, of the western world), but with the breaking of the medieval shell that both protected and confined it. The *ecclesia*, guardian of the apostolic preaching, the sacramental sign of Christ's presence in and to the world, is now free to serve a free society.

The Church and the political society, *sacerdotium* and *regnum*, enjoy, it is true, only a precarious freedom. It belongs to the mystery of human freedom that men, as citizens and as believers, can always sacrifice their freedom for a time. Our own age has witnessed such sacrifices on a scale greater, perhaps, than ever before in human history. But even in the depths of unfreedom, when we were tempted to think that the mystery of iniquity ruled over human fortunes, the dignity of human nature, and human capacity to find within its nature an authoritative rule of conduct, were vindicated. I should like here to cite the testimony of Dr. Dorota Lorska, a Polish Communist, at one time a prisoner in Auschwitz. She was a doctor; and she was asked, in the course of legal proceedings before a British Court, "whether, if she had been ordered to take part in experimental operations, she would have done so." In her reply she referred to what had been said by a fellow prisoner, a French woman doctor, Dr. Hautval. Dr. Hautval had said to her, after remarking that no one who had witnessed the medical experiments performed in the camp would be allowed to survive: "The only thing that is left for us is to behave, for the rest of the short time that is left to us, like human beings." Dr. Lorska added: "I have never forgotten that conversation and in all the difficult moments of my life I have remembered what she said to me."[10] This is to see the claims of morality as requirements of our human nature, and no more can be required of the citizen than this. That it is a stringent and costly requirement is sufficiently attested by the circumstances that called forth Dr. Hautval's classic utterance. This morality is given greater richness, though no greater stringency, if it is placed in its authentic context. It is that of the Hebrew Law and prophets, nothing of which is taken away by Christ who is their fulfilment. The particular oracles of the law often strike us as supreme commonplaces; but uttered in our own day, when the human family is so greatly threatened by the hatred of men for their neighbours and so degraded by a variety of superstitions, notably those of racialism, their edges are sharp. One such commonplace is worth repeating here. It has been a moral foundation of the growth of the people of the United States from their beginning and never disregarded without severe hurt to the nation; and it is a health-giving principle for all those living upon the planet

Earth. "When a stranger sojourns with you in your land, you shall not do him wrong. The stranger who sojourns with you shall be to you as the native among you, and you shall love him as yourself; for you were strangers in the land of Egypt" (Leviticus 19. 33, 34).

Notes

[1] For a magisterial treatment of this topic, see Ernst H. Kantorowicz, *The King's Two Bodies* (Princeton, N.J., 1957).

[2] "The command of a subordinate authority does not bind if it runs counter to the command of a superior in authority; as for instance, if the proconsul were to enjoin what the Emperor forbade." Saint Augustine, *Sermo VI De Verbis Domini*, c.8, cited in Eric D'Arcy, *Conscience and its Right to Freedom* (London and New York, 1961), p. 77.

[3] E.g. Reinhold Niebuhr, *Nations and Empires* (London, 1959).

[4] David Hume, *Enquiries concerning the Human Understanding and concerning the Principles of Morals*, ed. L. A. Selby-Bigge (2nd ed. Oxford, 1902), pp. 132-48 (*Enquiry concerning Human Understanding, Section* xi). *Hume's Dialogues concerning Natural Religion*, ed. Norman Kemp Smith (2nd ed. Edinburgh, 1947), passim.

[5] Sergius Bulgakov, *The Orthdox Church*, Eng. trans. Elizabeth S. Cram, ed. Donald A. Lowrie (London, 1935), pp. 162, 163.

[6] The distinction was employed in this way by many of the Catholic *bien pensants* who defended Pius XII against the criticisms implied in Hochhuth's play, *The Deputy*. Hochhuth's thought about one who claims to be a representative or vicar of the Transcendent, that this claim must, as it were, render itself perceptible, is close to my own. I do not suggest that his treatment of the very complex historical problem of the relation between Pius XII and the political powers of the Third Reich is either adequate or just.

[7] Vladimir Solovyev, *Russia and the Universal Church*, Eng. trans. Herbert Rees (London, 1948), p. 16. Italics added.

[8] Yves Congar O.P., "The Historical Development of Authority in the Church", in John M. Todd. ed., *Problems of Authority* (Baltimore and London, 1962), p. 140.

[9] J. Stevenson, ed., *A New Eusebius. Documents illustrative of the history of the Church to A.D. 337* (London, 1957), p. 60.

[10] *Codex Theodosianus*, xvi.1.2. A useful edition in translation is Clyde Pharr, trans., *The Theodosian Code* (Princeton, 1952). For an illuminating discussion of this edict, see Charles Norris Cochrane, *Christianity and Classical Culture* (New York, 1957), pp. 327 ff. Cochrane's great work was first published (in England) in an unfortunate year—1940—and has never received quite the measure of recognition it deserves.

[11] Immanuel Kant, *Critique of Pure Reason*, A 51, Eng. trans. Norman Kemp Smith (London, 1929), p. 93.

[12] Sir William Blackstone, *Commentaries on the Laws of England* (15th ed. 4 vols. with Notes and Additions by Edward Christian, London, 1809), *1*, 41. It is significant, and amusing, that Christian (Downing Professor of the Laws of England) is somewhat shocked by this thesis when it is presented in its full rigour. See, e.g., Christian's note, p. 41.

Notes

[13] Cited from the *De Legibus Angliae* in F. W. Maitland, *The Constitutional History of England* (Cambridge, 1919), pp. 100, 101

[14] Mark DeWolfe Howe, ed., *The Pollock-Holmes Letters* (2 vols. Cambridge, 1942), 2, 213.

CHAPTER II

[1] Cf. the interesting discussion in S. Z. Ehler, "On applying the modern term 'State' to the Middle Ages", *Medieval Studies presented to Aubrey Gwynn S.J.* (Dublin, 1961), pp. 492-501.

[2] See e.g. Michael Wilks, *The Problem of Sovereignty in the later Middle Ages* (Cambridge, 1963). Peter N. Riesenberg, *Inalienability of Sovereignty in Medieval Political Thought* (New York, 1956).

[3] For recent discussions of the problem of sovereignty, see H. L. A. Hart, *The Concept of Law* (Oxford, 1961), and W. J. Rees, "The Theory of Sovereignty Restated", in Peter Laslett, ed., *Philosophy, Politics and Society* (Oxford, 1956), pp. 56-82.

[4] Ludwig Wittgenstein, *Philosophical Investigations*, Eng. trans. G. E. M. Anscombe (Oxford, 1953), 599, p. 156e.

[5] As e.g. polygamy among the primitive Mormons was repressed by the Federal Government. This is, incidentally, something of a curiosity, for this repression seems to tremble on the borderline between those acts of government that seem to interfere with the free practice of religion and those that put down antisocial practices.

[6] Thomas Aquinas, *Summa Theologiae*, Ia Q.96 a.iv.

[7] Ibid., Ia IIae Q.94 a.ii.

[8] Richard Hooker, "Of the Laws of Ecclesiastical Polity", I.viii. 5, in *The Works*, arranged John Keble, revised R. W. Church and F. Paget (7th ed. 3 vols. Oxford, 1888), I, 229.

[9] What follows has been influenced by the writings—too rare—of Mrs. Philippa Foot and by what I have heard her say. See especially "Moral Arguments", *Mind*, N.S., 67 (1958), 502 ff.; "Moral Beliefs", *Proceedings of the Aristotelian Society*, N.S., 59 (1959), 83 ff.; "Goodness and Choice", *The Aristotelian Society*, *Supplementary Volume* 35 (1961), 45 ff. I should like to add that she has no responsibility for what I write and may well think it is wrong.

[10] For a penetrating discussion of this thesis, see Peter Winch, "Nature and Convention", *Proceedings of the Aristotelian Society*, N.S., 60 (1960), 231 ff.

[11] That virtue is one could perhaps be disputed.

[12] Cf. R. F. Holland, "Morality and the Two Worlds Concept", *Proceedings of the Aristotelian Society*, N.S., 56 (1956), 45 ff. This deeply impressive paper has the best discussion known to me of "inwardness".

[13] G. E. M. Anscombe, *Intention* (Oxford, 1957), p. 78.

[14] Thomas Hobbes, *Leviathan*, reprinted from the edition of 1651 (Oxford, 1958), pp. 122, 123.

[15] Ibid., p. 114.

[16] *Republic* 618e.

[17] John Henry (Cardinal) Newman, *Apologia pro vita sua* (London and New York, 1955), p. 218.

[18] *De civitate Dei*, XIX.c.vi. This is a somewhat free translation.

CHAPTER III

[1] J. Stevenson, ed., *A New Eusebius*, p. 262.

[2] Mark 16. 19; Acts 2. 33; Hebrews 10. 12; 12. 2.

[3] Cf. Heinrich Schlier, *Principalities and Powers in the New Testament* (Freiburg and London, 1961).

[4] Cf. "[The Church] is not just a group of people within the world, she is a new world. The sacramental world which we enter through baptism is a distinct new creation dating from the time of Christ's resurrection." Herbert McCabe O.P., *The New Creation* (London, 1964), p. 59. I am much indebted to this work, as also to E. Schillebeeckx O.P., *Christ the Sacrament of Encounter with God* (London, 1963).

[5] "And Christ really did become thoroughly *sarx*; the Word, says St. John, was made flesh (*sarx*); that is, he became man not merely in the sense of 'human being', but man in the existential condition of the children of Adam. Becoming man, God the Son entered into a humanity that had made its history one of condemnation, and that was branded with the sign of disobedience and alienation from God: death." Schillebeeckx, *Christ the Sacrament*, p. 29.

[6] Schillebeeckx, *Christ the Sacrament*, p. 14.

[7] This is not to suggest that the union of humanity with the Eternal Word takes place only when Christ is glorified. Christ always is *unus autem, non conversione Divinitatis in carnem: sed assumptione humanitatis in Deum* (Athanasian Creed).

[8] For the concept of sacrament, see McCabe, *The New Creation*, and Schillebeeckx, *Christ the Sacrament*. A thorough and scholarly account from a more "scholastic" standpoint is Bernard Leeming S.J., *Principles of Sacramental Theology* (London, 1956). For a searching discussion of sacramental piety, see Karl Rahner, "Personal and Sacramental Piety", in *Theological Investigations*, Eng. trans. Karl-H. Kruger (London and Baltimore, 1963), 2, 109-134.

[9] On this formula, see Schillebeeckx, *Christ the Sacrament*, pp. 82-88.

[10] "Freedom from symbols and articles is abstractedly the highest state of Christian communion", for ideally "the mysteries of divine truth . . . are kept hidden in the bosom of the Church . . . and reserved by a private teaching". John Henry Cardinal Newman, *The Arians of the Fourth Century* (5th ed. London, 1883), pp. 36, 37.

[11] This is done by Origen, Hippolytus, and Tertullian. See T. W. Manson, *Ministry and Priesthood: Christ's and Ours* (London, 1958), p. 43.

[12] E.g. by Manson.

[13] Cited by Congar in *Problems of Authority*, p. 126.

[14] Schillebeeckx, *Christ the Sacrament*, pp. 249, 250.

Notes

[15] Cited in C. R. Cheney and W. H. Semple, eds., *Selected Letters of Pope Innocent III concerning England* (London, 1953), p. xi.

[16] Some may think this a bit strong; but it is interesting to note the explicit Byzantinism of Stephen Gardiner in his Henrician period. See Pierre Janelle, ed., *Obedience in Church and State. Three Political Tracts by Stephen Gardiner* (Cambridge, 1930), pp. 116-19.

[17] *Codex Theodosianus*, xvi.1.2.

[18] Lord Acton, "The Protestant Theory of Persecution", in *Essays on Freedom and Power* (London, 1956), p. 132.

[19] Oscar Cullmann, *The State in the New Testament* (London, 1957), pp. 25 ff. I have in the main accepted Cullmann's interpretation of the New Testament evidence.

[20] I do not know if these young men were Christians, or if any of them was. But see Matthew 25. 31-45.

CHAPTER IV

[1] "The History of Freedom in Christianity", in Lord Acton, *Essays on Freedom and Power*, p. 91.

[2] Ibid., p. 87.

[3] Whitehead speaks of "the greatest contribution of medievalism to the formation of the scientific movement" as being "the inexpugnable belief that every detailed occurrence can be correlated with its antecedents in a perfectly definite manner, exemplifying general principles.... How has this conviction been so vividly implanted in the European mind? ... It must come from the medieval insistence on the rationality of God, conceived as with the personal energy of Jehovah and with the rationality of a Greek philosopher . . . faith in the possibility of science, generated antecedently to the development of modern scientific theory, is an unconscious derivative from medieval theology". A. N. Whitehead, *Science and the Modern World* (Cambridge, 1932), pp. 15, 16. I believe the first person to emphasize the "secularism" of Franciscan thought was Mr. Christopher Dawson. See, for instance, his *Progress and Religion* (London, 1929), pp. 170, 171.

[4] Cf. the many original and penetrating remarks by Dietrich Bonhoeffer in *Letters and Papers from Prison* (London, 1959), especially pp. 77-79 and pp. 106 ff. I do not think Bonhoeffer here or elsewhere offers satisfactory solutions to the problems he raises; but his great merit is to have raised the problems.

[5] This, like so much else, was anticipated by the sectarians of the English Civil War, e.g. "Every man by nature being a King, Priest and Prophet in his owne naturall circuit and compasse. . . ." Richard Overton, *An Arrow against all Tyrants* (1646), cited in C. B. Macpherson, *The Political Theory of Possessive Individualism* (Oxford, 1962), pp. 140, 141.

[6] This is the thesis of Will Herberg concerning much religiosity in the United States. See his *Protestant-Catholic-Jew* (new and revised ed. New York, 1960), especially pp. 254-72.

[7] This is the characteristic confusion of the bourgeoisie so memorably diagnosed by Kierkegaard. "Morality is to them the highest, far more important than intelligence; but they have never felt enthusiasm for greatness, for talent even though in its abnormal form. Their *ethics* are a short summary of police ordinances; for them the most important thing is to be a useful member of the state, and to air their opinions in the club of an evening; they have never felt homesickness for something unknown and far away, nor the depth which consists in being nothing at all, of walking out of Nørreport with a penny in one's pocket and a cane in one's hand." *The Journals of Søren Kierkegaard*, A Selection edited and translated by Alexander Dru (London, 1938), pp. 49, 50.

[8] H. I. Marrou, *A History of Education in Antiquity*, trans. George Lamb (London, 1956), pp. 316, 317. I have relied on Marrou's account of the Christian attitude to the pagan school. I am indebted to my colleague Mr. T. C. Potts for drawing my attention to Marrou's work.

[9] *Mater et Magistra*, trans. H. E. Winstone (revised ed. London, 1962), paras. 106, 107 (pp. 30, 31). Italics added.

[10] *Dering v. Uris and others, The Times* (London) (April 29, 1964).

Index

124

Index